Megan

What a fun and exciting year of confirmation!!!
It was such a treat getting to know you.
We thoroughly enjoyed our year of bible study
and especially the weekend of our retreat.
Can't wait for next year's boot hockey game!

While you are enjoying your summer
break, we hope you take a moment
each week to read this book.

We hope it further strengthens your
spiritual life and raises questions for
you to think about and make good choices.

Enjoy!!

Wendy Toenies and Even Rigstad
Confirmation Guides

SOCIAL NETWORKING

100 Days To See Where GOD Fits In!

The quoted ideas expressed in this book (but not Scripture verses) are not, in all cases, exact quotations, as some have been edited for clarity and brevity. In all cases, the author has attempted to maintain the speaker's original intent. In some cases, quoted material for this book was obtained from secondary sources, primarily print media. While every effort was made to ensure the accuracy of these sources, the accuracy cannot be guaranteed. For additions, deletions, corrections, or clarifications in future editions of this text, please write Freeman-Smith, LLC.

Scripture quotations are taken from:

The Holy Bible, King James Version

The Holy Bible, New International Version (NIV) Copyright © 1973, 1978, 1984, by International Bible Society. Used by permission of Zondervan Publishing House. All rights reserved.

The New American Standard Bible®, (NASB) Copyright © 1960, 1962, 1963, 1968, 1971, 1972, 1973, 1975, 1977, 1995 by The Lockman Foundation. Used by permission.

The Holy Bible, New King James Version (NKJV) Copyright © 1982 by Thomas Nelson, Inc. Used by permission.

The Holy Bible, New Living Translation, (NLT) Copyright © 1996. Used by permission of Tyndale House Publishers, Inc., Wheaton, Illinois 60189. All rights reserved.

New Century Version®. (NCV) Copyright © 1987, 1988, 1991 by Word Publishing, a division of Thomas Nelson, Inc. All rights reserved. Used by permission.

The Message (MSG) This edition issued by contractual arrangement with NavPress, a division of The Navigators, U.S.A. Originally published by NavPress in English as THE MESSAGE: The Bible in Contemporary Language copyright 2002-2003 by Eugene Peterson. All rights reserved.

The Holman Christian Standard Bible™ (HOLMAN CSB) Copyright © 1999, 2000, 2001 by Holman Bible Publishers. Used by permission.

Cover Design by Kim Russell / Wahoo Designs
Page Layout by Bart Dawson

ISBN 978-1-60587-100-4

Printed in the United States of America

TO

_____

FROM

_____

SOCIAL NETWORKING

100 Days To See Where GOD Fits In!

Introduction

I n the old days, social networking was so much simpler. It was done face-to-face, or maybe by phone, or by snail mail. And that was about it.

But no more.

Today, you can stay in constant contact with friends or strangers by using a dizzying array of digital platforms that, only a few years ago, might have seemed like science fiction. Maybe you're on Facebook. Maybe you Tweet. Or text. Maybe your videos are on YouTube, and maybe your band is on MySpace. Or maybe you're using some other digital means of staying in touch with your buddies and with the world. But how does your faith fit into this social network? And how can you be sure that God is pleased with your content?

This book offers 100 quick devotionals that are inteneded to help you think about your own social network, and about where God fits in. These are good things to think about because the digital world offers limitless opportunities to stray from the path that God intends for your life. It's far easier to get caught up in the digital quicksand than it is to get out of it.

Every day, when you log onto your network, you are confronted with temptations and distractions that were totally unknown to previous generations. Your world is changing so rapidly that, at times, it may seem difficult to catch your breath and keep your balance. So, if you're smart, you'll ask for God's guidance many times each day . . . starting with a regular morning devotional. When you do, you will soon find yourself making wise choices—choices that will improve your day, enhance your social network, and, quite literally, revolutionize your life.

Social Networks Force You to Make Choices, So Choose Wisely

*The thing you should want most is God's kingdom
and doing what God wants.
Then all these other things you need will be given to you.*

Matthew 6:33 NCV

Choices, choices, choices! Whether you're trying to figure out which photos to load into Facebook or trying to decide whether to hit the send button on some testy text message, you've got lots of choices to make in the digital world. And sometimes, making those choices isn't easy. At times you're torn between what you want to do (impress your friends) and what you ought to do (obey your Creator). When that happens, it's up to you to choose wisely . . . or else.

The social networking choices you make today can make a really big difference in the quality of your life now and in the future. When you make wise choices, you are rewarded; when you make unwise choices, you must accept the consequences. It's as simple as that. So make sure that your choices are pleasing to God . . . or else.

No matter how many books you read, no matter
how many schools you attend, you're never really wise
until you start making wise choices.

Marie T. Freeman

Life is a series of choices between
the bad, the good, and the best.
Everything depends on how we choose.

Vance Havner

Social Networking Common Sense: Figure out how different sites work before you decide which sites to join. Some sites will allow only a predefined community of users to download or post content while other sites allow anyone and everyone to view and post. If you're not sure where to get started, consider starting out with a small, safe, friendly group of users.

Put God First

Do not have other gods besides Me.
Exodus 20:3 Holman CSB

Who is really in charge of your social network? Is it God, or is it somebody else? Have you given God first place in every aspect of your life (including your digital life), or are you giving Him little more than a few hours each Sunday morning?

In the book of Exodus, God warns that we should place no gods before Him. Yet all too often, we place our Lord in second, third, or fourth place as we worship other things. When we unwittingly place possessions or relationships above our love for the Creator, we create big problems for ourselves.

Have you chosen to allow God to rule your heart? Make certain that the honest answer to this question is a resounding yes. In the life of every thoughtful believer, God comes first. And that's precisely the place that He deserves in your heart.

One with God is a majority.

Billy Graham

God is the beyond in the midst of our life.

Dietrich Bonhoeffer

You can't get second things by putting them first;
you can get second things
only by putting first things first.

C. S. Lewis

Something to Think About: You should put God first in every aspect of your life, including your social network. God deserves to come first, and you deserve the experience of putting Him first.

Trying to Please Too Many People Can Lead to Big Trouble

Don't become partners with those who reject God.
How can you make a partnership out of right and wrong?
That's not partnership; that's war.
Is light best friends with dark?

2 Corinthians 6:14 MSG

Okay, you're ready to upload a posting or send a text. Before you push send, here's a question worth asking yourself: Are you a people-pleaser or a God-pleaser? Hopefully, you're far more concerned with pleasing God than you are with pleasing your friends. But face facts: even if you're a devoted Christian, you're still going to feel the urge to impress your friends and acquaintances—and sometimes that urge will be strong.

Peer pressure can be good or bad, depending upon who your peers are and how they behave. If your friends encourage you to follow God's will and to obey His commandments, then you'll experience positive peer pressure, and that's a good thing. But, if your friends encourage you to do foolish things, then you're facing a different kind of peer pressure . . . and you'd better beware.

To sum it up, here's your choice: you can choose to please God first, or you can fall victim to peer pressure. The choice is yours—and so are the consequences.

> If you choose to awaken a passion for God,
> you will have to choose your friends wisely.
>
> Lisa Bevere

> Those who follow the crowd usually get lost in it.
>
> Rick Warren

Something to Think About: If you try too hard to please other people (instead of trying to please God) you may find yourself making unwise choices.

Standing Up for Your Beliefs

Souls who follow their hearts thrive;
fools bent on evil despise matters of soul.

Proverbs 13:19 MSG

It's not enough to be a Christian on Sunday mornings. You should also be willing to demonstrate your faith online, and everywhere else, for that matter.

If you're willing to stand up for the things you believe in, you'll make better choices. But if you're one person on Sunday morning and a different person throughout the rest of the week, you'll be doing yourself—and your conscience—a big disservice.

The moment that you decide to stand up for your beliefs, you can no longer be a lukewarm, halfhearted Christian. And, when you are no longer a lukewarm Christian, God rejoices (and the devil doesn't).

So stand up for your beliefs. And remember this: in the battle of good versus evil, the devil never takes a day off . . . and neither should you.

God's presence is with you, but you have to make
a choice to believe—and I mean, really believe—
that this is true. This conscious decision is yours alone.

Bill Hybels

Jesus taught that the evidence that confirms our leaps of
faith comes after we risk believing, not before.

Gloria Gaither

What I believe about God
is the most important thing about me.

A. W. Tozer

Something to Think About: When you stand up for your
beliefs, whether you're online or anywhere else, you'll make
better choices.

You're Worth It!

You're blessed when you're content with just who you are—
no more, no less. That's the moment you find yourselves
proud owners of everything that can't be bought.

Matthew 5:5 MSG

The Internet can be a discouraging place where idle gossip and negative feedback can tear down your self-esteem in a hurry. Of course, you've probably been told plenty of times that you're special: special to God, special to your family, special to your friends, and a special addition to God's wonderful world! But sometimes, when your social network turns decidedly negative, you may not feel very special. In fact, you may decide that you're the ugliest duckling in the digital pond, a not-very-special person. And if you think that, you're mistaken.

The Bible says that God made you in "an amazing and wonderful way." So the next time that you start feeling like you don't measure up, remember this: when God made all the people of the earth, He only made one you. You're incredibly valuable to Him, and that means that you should think of yourself as a V.I.P. God wants you to have the best, and you deserve the best . . . you're worth it!

You are valuable just because you exist.
Not because of what you do or what you have done,
but simply because you are.

Max Lucado

Human worth does not depend on beauty or intelligence
or accomplishments. We are all more valuable than
the possessions of the entire world simply because
God gave us that value.

James Dobson

Being loved by Him whose opinion matters most gives us
the security to risk loving, too—even loving ourselves.

Gloria Gaither

Social Networking Common Sense: It's smart to keep as much control as you can over the stuff you post and the eyeballs that are viewing it. So consider restricting access to your page to a select group of people, for example, your friends from church, or your school, or your team, or your family.

The Choice to Study God's Word

All Scripture is inspired by God and is profitable for teaching,
for rebuking, for correcting, for training in righteousness,
so that the man of God may be complete,
equipped for every good work.

2 Timothy 3:16-17 Holman CSB

Maybe you're spending lots of time texting, posting, scanning, sending, and networking. If so, you're reading lots and lots of content courtesy of the digital world. So how much time are you spending reading God's messages? Do you read your Bible a lot . . . or not? The answer to this simple question will determine, to a surprising extent, the quality of your decisions, the quality of your life, and the direction of your faith.

You (and only you) must decide whether God's Word will be a bright spotlight that guides your path every day or a tiny nightlight that occasionally flickers in the dark. The decision to study the Bible—or not—is an important choice; how you choose to use your Bible will have a profound impact on your future.

The Bible is unlike any other book. It is a priceless gift from your Creator, a tool that God intends for you to use in every aspect of your life. And, it contains promises upon which you, as a Christian, can and must depend.

God's Word can be a roadmap to success and spiritual abundance. Make it your roadmap. God's wisdom can be a light to guide your steps. Claim it as your light today, tomorrow, and every day of your life—and then walk confidently in the footsteps of God's only begotten Son.

Some read the Bible to learn,
and some read the Bible to hear from heaven.

Andrew Murray

Something to Think About: If you want to know God, you should take time to read the book He wrote. It's at the bookstore; it's online; it's probably on your bookshelf. And it has eternal consequences for you.

Following Jesus Today and Every Day

Then He said to them all,
"If anyone wants to come with Me, he must deny himself,
take up his cross daily, and follow Me."
Luke 9:23 Holman CSB

With whom will you walk today? Will you walk with shortsighted people who honor the ways of the world, or will you walk with the Son of God? Jesus walks with you. Are you walking with Him? Hopefully, you will choose to walk with Him today and every day of your life.

Jesus doesn't want you to be a run-of-the-mill, follow-the-crowd kind of person. Jesus wants you to be a "new creation" through Him. And that's exactly what you should want for yourself, too. Nothing is more important than your wholehearted commitment to your Creator and to His only begotten Son. Your faith must never be an afterthought; it must be your ultimate priority, your ultimate possession, and your ultimate passion.

You are the recipient of Christ's love. Accept it enthusiastically and share it passionately. Jesus deserves your extreme enthusiasm; the world deserves it; and you deserve the experience of sharing it.

Will you, with a glad and eager surrender,
hand yourself and all that concerns you over into his
hands? If you will do this, your soul will begin to know
something of the joy of union with Christ.

Hannah Whitall Smith

Social Networking Common Sense: Never post anything on the web that you wouldn't be proud for the whole world to see, including your parents. And the same goes for your texts and Tweets.

Picking the Right Social Network

Iron sharpens iron, and one man sharpens another.

Proverbs 27:17 Holman CSB

Because we tend to become like our friends, we must choose our friends carefully, and that includes the friends we make online. Our friends influence us in ways that are both subtle and powerful, so we must ensure that our friendships honor God. Because our friends have the power to lift us up or to bring us down, we must select friends who, by their words and their actions, encourage us to lead Christ-centered lives.

When we build lasting friendships that are pleasing to God, we are blessed. When we seek out encouraging friends and mentors, they lift us up. And, when we make ourselves a powerful source of encouragement to others, we do God's work here on earth.

Do you seek to be a godly Christian? If so, you should build friendships that honor your Creator. When you do, God will bless you and your friends, today and forever.

We, as God's people, are not only to stay far away
from sin and sinners who would entice us,
but we are to be so like our God that we mourn over sin.

Kay Arthur

The best times in life are made a thousand times better
when shared with a dear friend.

Luci Swindoll

A friend is one who makes me do my best.

Oswald Chambers

Something to Think About: You'll probably end up behaving like your friends behave . . . and if that's a scary thought, it's time to make a new set of friends.

Choosing the Direction of Your Thoughts

There is one thing I always do.
Forgetting the past and straining toward what is ahead,
I keep trying to reach the goal and get the prize
for which God called me . . . .

Philippians 3:13–14 NCV

The digital world can shape your thoughts and reprogram your brain if you let it. Don't let it. Instead of letting the world control your thoughts, ask God to guide them.

Jesus taught us that a pure heart is a wonderful blessing. It's up to each of us to fill our hearts with love for God, love for Jesus, and love for all people. When we do, good things happen.

Sometimes, of course, we don't feel much like feeling good. Sometimes, when we're tired, or frustrated, or angry, we simply don't want to have a good attitude. On those days when we're feeling bad, it's time to calm down . . . and rest up.

Do you want to be the best person you can be? Then you shouldn't grow tired of doing the right things . . . and you shouldn't ever grow tired of thinking the right thoughts.

The Reference Point for the Christian is the Bible. All values, judgments, and attitudes must be gauged in relationship to this Reference Point.

Ruth Bell Graham

You've heard the saying, "Life is what you make it." That means we have a choice. We can choose to have a life full of frustration and fear, but we can just as easily choose one of joy and contentment.

Dennis Swanberg

Something to Think About: You have the power to choose the direction of your thoughts. Good thoughts lead to good results; bad thoughts lead elsewhere.

Avoiding All Those Temptations

Put on the whole armor of God, that you may be able to stand against the wiles of the devil.

Ephesians 6:11 NKJV

The Internet can be a dangerous place. And social networks can be good or bad, depending upon how they are used. Yep, here in the 21st century, the bad guys are working around the clock to lead you astray. That's why you must remain vigilant.

In a letter to believers, Peter offers a stern warning: "Your adversary, the devil, prowls around like a roaring lion, seeking someone to devour" (1 Peter 5:8 NASB). What was true in New Testament times is equally true in our own. Satan tempts his prey and then devours them (and it's up to you—and only you—to make sure that you're not one of the ones being devoured!).

As a believer who seeks a genuine relationship with Jesus, you must beware because temptations are everywhere, including online. Satan is determined to win; you must be equally determined that he does not.

Jesus faced every temptation known to humanity
so that He could identify with us.

Beth Moore

Our battles are first won or lost in the secret places
of our will in God's presence,
never in full view of the world.

Oswald Chambers

Flee temptation without leaving a forwarding address.

Barbara Johnson

Social Networking Common Sense: Temptations are everywhere, especially in the digital universe. It's your job to avoid them . . . or else!

Think B4 U Click

Knowing God leads to self-control.
Self-control leads to patient endurance,
and patient endurance leads to godliness.

2 Peter 1:6 NLT

Would you like a winning formula for making smart choices, whether you're inside your social network or outside it? Okay, here's that formula: Think about things first and do things next, not vice versa.

Are you, at times, just a little bit too impulsive? Do you react first (and dash off a hasty message) and think about that message later? If so, God wants to have a little chat with you.

God's Word is clear: as a believer, you are called to lead a life of discipline, diligence, moderation, and maturity. But the world often tempts you to behave otherwise. Everywhere you turn, or so it seems, the world encourages you to act impulsively. But God wants you to act wisely. Trust God.

The effective Christians of history have been men and women of great personal discipline—mental discipline, discipline of the body, discipline of the tongue, and discipline of the emotion.

Billy Graham

Love, joy, peace, patience, kindness, goodness, faithfulness, gentleness, and self-control.
To these I commit my day. If I succeed, I will give thanks. If I fail, I will seek his grace. And then, when this day is done, I will place my head on my pillow and rest.

Max Lucado

Social Networking Common Sense: Think things through before you press the send button, not after. If you're too impulsive, you may send a text or make a post that you might regret later. So when in doubt, slow down. Think b4 u click.

Maxing Your Talent

I remind you to fan into flame the gift of God.

2 Timothy 1:6 NIV

You've got an array of talents that need to be refined, and it takes time to refine those talents. But if you're spending all day texting and posting, how can you improve your skills? The answer is, you can't.

All people possess special gifts—bestowed from the Father above—and you are no exception. It takes time for you to find your particular gift and it must be cultivated—by you—or it will go unused . . . and God's gift to you will be squandered.

Are you willing to do the hard work that's required to discover your talents and to develop them? If you are wise, you'll answer "yes." After all, if you don't make the most of your talents, who has the most to lose? You do!

So make a promise to yourself that you will earnestly seek to discover the talents that God has given you. Then, nourish those talents and make them grow. Finally, vow to share your gifts with the world for as long as God gives you the power to do so. After all, the best way to say "Thank You" for God's gifts is to use them.

God often reveals His direction for our lives through
the way He made us, with a certain
personality and unique skills.

Bill Hybels

You are the only person on earth
who can use your ability.

Zig Ziglar

You are a unique blend of talents, skills, and gifts,
which makes you an indispensable member
of the body of Christ.

Charles Stanley

Something to Think About: You have talents and opportunities which you can choose to use . . . or not. You must either use them or lose them.

Give God Your Complete Attention

Worship the Lord your God and . . . serve Him only.
Matthew 4:10 Holman CSB

When a text message or a post comes your way, you pay attention. But are you also paying attention to God? Let's hope so, because it's a dangerous world out there, so you need God's guidance and protection.

Nineteenth century clergyman Edwin Hubbel Chapin warned, "Neutral men are the devil's allies." His words were true then, and they're true now. Neutrality in the face of evil is a sin. Yet all too often, we fail to fight evil, not because we are neutral, but because we are shortsighted: we don't fight the devil because we don't recognize his handiwork.

If we are to recognize evil and fight it, we must pay careful attention. We must pay attention to God's Word, and we must pay attention to the realities of everyday life. When we observe life objectively, and when we do so with eyes and hearts that are attuned to God's Holy Word, we can no longer be neutral believers. And when we are no longer neutral, God rejoices while the devil despairs.

Don't be a half-Christian. There are too many of them in the world already. The world has a profound respect for a person who is sincere in his faith.

Billy Graham

I need the spiritual revival that comes from spending quiet time alone with Jesus in prayer and in thoughtful meditation on His Word.

Anne Graham Lotz

Something to Think About: Having trouble hearing God? Put down the cell phone, shut down the computer, and try spending a little more time in silence. Sometimes God speaks in a quiet voice, and if your world is too noisy, you might miss some of His most important messages.

Texting Respectfully and Responsibly

Pleasant words are a honeycomb:
sweet to the taste and health to the body.

Proverbs 16:24 Holman CSB

Want a social network that pleases God? A great place to start is by guarding your words. And make no mistake—you'll feel better about yourself if you pay careful attention to the things you text and the things you post. Of course you must never take the Lord's name in vain, but it doesn't stop there. You must also try to speak words of encouragement, words that lift others up, words that give honor to your Heavenly Father.

When you're frustrated or tired, you may type things that would be better left un-typed. And whenever you lash out in anger, you miss a wonderful opportunity—the opportunity to consider your messages before you send them. A far better strategy, of course, is to do the more difficult thing: to think first and to communicate next. When you do, you give yourself more time to compose your thoughts and to consult your Creator (but not necessarily in that order!).

Ephesians 4:29 instructs you to make "each word a gift" (MSG). These passages make it clear that God cares very much about the things you say and the way you say them. And if God cares that much, so should you.

The great test of a man's character is his tongue.
Oswald Chambers

Change the heart, and you change the speech.
Warren Wiersbe

A little kindly advice is better than
a great deal of scolding.
Fanny Crosby

Social Networking Common Sense: Remember that text messages and web postings can be saved permanently by friends and foes alike. So be very careful about the things you text and the things you post.

Conforming Your Digital Priorities to God's Priorities

Come near to God, and God will come near to you.
You sinners, clean sin out of your lives.
You who are trying to follow God and the world
at the same time, make your thinking pure.

James 4:8 NCV

Okay, there's simply not enough time in the day to keep up with all your friends, do all your schoolwork, and grab a few hours of sleep every night. So what's a person to do? Well, a great place to start is by asking God for some help.

Have you ever asked God to help prioritize your life? Have you asked Him for guidance and for the courage to do the things that you know need to be done (and to say no the things that don't)? If so, then you're continually inviting your Creator to reveal Himself in a variety of ways.

When you make God's priorities your priorities, you will receive God's abundance and His peace. When you make God a full partner in every aspect of your life, He will lead you along the proper path: His path. When you allow God to reign over your heart, He will honor you with spiritual blessings that are simply too numerous to count. So, as you plan for the day ahead, make God's will your ultimate priority. When you do, every other priority will have a tendency to fall neatly into place.

Give God what's right—not what's left!

Anonymous

With God, it's never "Plan B" or "second best."
It's always "Plan A." And, if we let Him,
He'll make something beautiful of our lives.

Gloria Gaither

Something to Think About: FYI: Your time is limited, so your social network should be, too. You simply don't have time to communicate with everybody on planet earth. So it's perfectly okay to say no to the things that mean less so that you'll have time for the things that mean more.

Avoiding Gossip

So rid yourselves of all wickedness,
all deceit, hypocrisy, envy, and all slander.
I Peter 2:1 Holman CSB

It's true: gossip is the guilty little pleasure that tempts almost all of us from time to time. Why is it so tempting to gossip? Because when we put other people down, we experience a brief dose of self-righteousness as we look down our noses at the supposed misdeeds of others. But there's a catch: in truth, we can never really build ourselves up by tearing other people down. So the habit of gossip turns out to be a self-defeating waste of time.

It's no wonder that the Bible clearly teaches that gossip is wrong. Consider the simple advice found in Proverbs 16:28: "Gossip ruins friendships" (NCV). So do yourself a big favor: don't spend precious time talking about other people. It's a waste of words, it's the wrong thing to do, and in the end, it will leave you with less self-respect, not more.

Online gossiping is easy, but it's wrong. So don't become entangled in a network that says bad things—or untrue things—about others. When you avoid the temptation to engage in gossip, you'll feel better about yourself—and other people will feel better about you, too.

Kindness in this world will do much to help others,
not only to come into the light,
but also to grow in grace day by day.

Fanny Crosby

Christians think they are prosecuting attorneys or
judges, when, in reality,
God has called all of us to be witnesses.

Warren Wiersbe

To belittle is to be little.

Anonymous

Something to Think About: When texting or talking about other people, use this guideline: don't ever say something behind someone's back that you wouldn't say to that person directly.

Look for Fulfillment in the Right Places

I am the Gate. Anyone who goes through me will be cared for—will freely go in and out, and find pasture. A thief is only there to steal and kill and destroy. I came so they can have real and eternal life, more and better life than they ever dreamed of. I am the Good Shepherd. The Good Shepherd puts the sheep before himself, sacrifices himself if necessary.

John 10:9-11 MSG

Where can we find contentment? Can we find it online? Or by social networking? Is contentment the result of wealth, or power, or beauty, or fame? Nope. Genuine contentment is a gift from God to those who trust Him and follow His commandments.

Our modern world seems preoccupied with the search for happiness. We are bombarded with messages telling us that happiness depends upon the acquisition of material possessions. These messages are false. Enduring peace is not the result of our acquisitions; it is a spiritual gift from God to those who obey Him and accept His will.

If we don't find contentment in God, we will never find it anywhere else. But, if we seek Him and obey Him, we will be blessed with an inner peace that is beyond human understanding. When God dwells at the center of our lives, peace and contentment will belong to us just as surely as we belong to God.

We will never be happy until we make God the source of our fulfillment and the answer to our longings.

Stormie Omartian

God's riches are beyond anything we could ask or even dare to imagine! If my life gets gooey and stale, I have no excuse.

Barbara Johnson

Something to Think About: If you're not content, try focusing less on "stuff" and more on God.

Choosing to Be a Cheerful Christian

The cheerful heart has a continual feast.

Proverbs 15:15 NIV

Whether you're texting a message, hanging out in a chat room, or posting a comment online, it pays to be a cheerful Christian. After all, Christ promises us lives of abundance and joy, but He does not force His joy upon us. We must claim His joy for ourselves, and when we do, Jesus, in turn, fills our spirits with His power and His love.

How can we receive from Christ the joy that is rightfully ours? By giving Him what is rightfully His: our hearts and our souls.

When we earnestly commit ourselves to the Savior of mankind, when we place Jesus at the center of our lives and trust Him as our personal Savior, He will transform us, not just for today, but for all eternity. Then we, as God's children, can share Christ's joy and His message with a world that needs both.

God is good, and heaven is forever.
And if those two facts don't cheer you up, nothing will.

Marie T. Freeman

Sour godliness is the devil's religion.

John Wesley

The people whom I have seen succeed best in life have
always been cheerful and hopeful people who went about
their business with a smile on their faces.

Charles Kingsley

Something to Think About: Do you need a little cheering
up? If so, find somebody else who needs cheering up, too.
Then, do your best to brighten that person's day. When you
do, you'll discover that cheering up other people is a wonderful way to cheer yourself up, too!

Avoid People Who Behave Foolishly

Do not be misled: "Bad company corrupts good character."

1 Corinthians 15:33 NIV

It's true whether you're online or in person: If you hang out with people who do dumb things, pretty soon, you'll probably find yourself doing dumb things, too. And that's bad . . . very bad. So here's an ironclad rule for earning more self-respect and more rewards from life: If your social network is headed in the wrong direction, find another peer group, and fast. Otherwise, before you know it, you'll be caught up in trouble that you didn't create and you don't deserve.

When you feel pressured to do things—or to say things—that lead you away from God, you're heading straight for trouble. So don't do the "easy" thing or the "popular" thing. Do the right thing, and don't worry about winning any popularity contests.

Inasmuch as anyone pushes you nearer to God,
he or she is your friend.

Barbara Johnson

True friends don't spend time gazing into each other's
eyes. They show great tenderness toward each other, but
they face in the same direction, toward common projects,
interest, goals, and above all, toward a common Lord.

C. S. Lewis

We, as God's people, are not only to stay far away from sin
and sinners who would entice us, but we are to be so like
our God that we mourn over sin.

Kay Arthur

Social Networking Common Sense: Don't assume that all
the kids you meet online are kids. They may actually be
adults (yuk!). So be careful, and never give out personal
info.

Let God Be Your Guide

The true children of God are those who let God's Spirit lead them.

Romans 8:14 NCV

Are you trying to figure out what to say, what to post, or whom to include in your social network? The Bible promises that God will guide you if you let Him. Your job is to let Him. But sometimes, you will be tempted to do otherwise. Sometimes, you'll be tempted to go along with the crowd; other times, you'll be tempted to do things your way, not God's way. When you feel these temptations, resist them.

God has promised that when you ask for His help, He will not withhold it. So ask. Ask Him to meet the needs of your day. Ask Him to lead you, to protect you, and to correct you. And trust the answers He gives.

God stands at the door and waits. When you knock, He opens. When you ask, He answers. Your task, of course, is to seek His guidance prayerfully, confidently, and often.

We must always invite Jesus to be the navigator
of our plans, desires, wills, and emotions,
for He is the way, the truth, and the life.

Bill Bright

God often reveals His direction for our lives through
the way He made us . . .
with a certain personality and unique skills.

Bill Hybels

God's leading will never be contrary to His word.

Vonette Bright

Something to Think About: If you want to be a little more
like Christ . . . learn about His teachings, follow in His
footsteps, and obey His commandments.

Addicted?

Be sober! Be on the alert!
Your adversary the Devil is prowling around like
a roaring lion, looking for anyone he can devour.

1 Peter 5:8 Holman CSB

Some people text so much that their thumbs go numb. Others stay online so long that their eyes glaze over. And still others spend more time gaming than they do sleeping. Are these folks suffering from digital addiction? That's up for debate, but here's something you can be sure of: If you want to wreck your life, get addicted to something that destroys your health or your sanity. If (God forbid) you allow yourself to become addicted to any earthly temptation, you're steering straight for a boatload of negative consequences, not to mention a big bad dose of negative self-esteem.

Unless you're living on a deserted island, you know people who are full-blown addicts—probably lots of people. It's up to you to make certain that you don't become one of them.

To many, total abstinence is easier
than perfect moderation.

St. Augustine

Virtue—even attempted virtue—brings light;
indulgence brings fog.

C. S. Lewis

Addiction is the most powerful psychic enemy of
humanity's desire for God.

Gerald May

Something to Think About: Remember that ultimately you
and you alone are responsible for the way you spend your
time. Others may warn you, help you, or encourage you, but
in the end, the habits that rule your life are the very same
habits that you yourself have formed.

Finding Worthwhile Things You Can Be Passionate About

Whatever you do, do all to the glory of God.

1 Corinthians 10:31 NKJV

I t's easy to get wrapped up in social networking, but please don't forget that there's a real world out there, a world that needs competent, enthusiastic, hardworking Christians (like you).

Can you honestly say that you are an enthusiastic person? Are you passionate about your faith and excited about your path? Hopefully so. But if your zest for life has waned, it is now time to redirect your efforts and recharge your spiritual batteries. And that means refocusing your priorities by putting God first.

Nothing is more important than your wholehearted commitment to your Creator and to His only begotten Son. Your faith must never be an afterthought; it must be your ultimate priority, your ultimate possession, and your ultimate passion.

When the dream of our heart is one that God has planted there, a strange happiness flows into us. At that moment, all of the spiritual resources of the universe are released to help us. Our praying is then at one with the will of God and becomes a channel for the Creator's purposes for us and our world.

Catherine Marshall

When we wholeheartedly commit ourselves to God, there is nothing mediocre or run-of-the-mill about us. To live for Christ is to be passionate about our Lord and about our lives.

Jim Gallery

Something to Think About: Whether you're online or anywhere else, you should try to involve yourself in activities that you can support wholeheartedly and enthusiastically. It's easier to celebrate life when you're passionately involved in life.

Pray Early and Often

Be cheerful no matter what; pray all the time;
thank God no matter what happens. This is the way God
wants you who belong to Christ Jesus to live.

1 Thessalonians 5:16-18 MSG

Most people find enough time to text, but when it comes to finding time for prayer, well, that's another matter entirely.

Perhaps, because of all the stuff you're doing, you've neglected to pay sufficient attention to a particularly important part of your life: the spiritual part. If so, today is the day to change, and one way to make that change is simply to spend a little more time talking with God.

God is trying to get His message through to you. Are you listening?

Perhaps, on occasion, you may find yourself overwhelmed by the pressures of everyday life. Perhaps you may forget to slow yourself down long enough to talk with God. Instead of turning your thoughts and prayers to Him, you may rely upon your own resources. Instead of asking God for guidance, you may (mistakenly) depend upon your social network to supply all the answers. A far better course of action is this: simply stop what you're doing long enough to open your heart to God; then listen carefully for His directions.

In all things great and small, seek God's wisdom and His grace. He hears your prayers, and He will answer. All you must do is ask.

> Some people pray just to pray,
> and some people pray to know God.
>
> Andrew Murray

> We are not to have faith in prayer,
> but in God who answers prayer.
>
> Anonymous

Something to Think About: When you are praying, the position of your eyelids makes little or no difference. Of course it's good to close your eyes and bow your head whenever you can, but it's also good to offer quick prayers to God with your eyes—and your heart—wide open.

Choosing to Face Up to Your Responsibilities

We want each of you to go on with the same hard work all your lives so you will surely get what you hope for. We do not want you to become lazy. Be like those who through faith and patience will receive what God has promised.

Hebrews 6:11–12 NCV

The Internet wouldn't be so dangerous if everybody acted responsibly. But they don't. Lots of people do dumb stuff on the Internet, and sometimes the bad guys out there do things that are intended to harm your heart and tear down your faith.

So what are you supposed to do? You're supposed to (drum roll, please . . .) act responsibly.

The words from the sixth chapter of Hebrews remind us that as Christians we are instructed to be diligent, faithful, and responsible. And no exceptions are made for irresponsible activities that are conducted in the digital world.

Do you want to be a worthy example for your family and friends? If so, you must preach the gospel of responsible behavior, not only with your words, but also by your actions. Of course, it's not always easy to face up to your responsibilities, but it's always the right thing to do. So the next time you're faced with the choice of doing the right thing or the easy thing, do what's right. It's the truly decent way to live.

Every time you refuse to face up to life and its problems, you weaken your character.

E. Stanley Jones

Action springs not from thought, but from a readiness for responsibility.

Dietrich Bonhoeffer

Social Networking Common Sense: Use firewalls responsibly; be sure to put all your personal stuff behind password protected walls, where only your friends and family can view it.

Be Careful How You Spend Your Time . . . and Your Life

There is an occasion for everything,
and a time for every activity under heaven.
Ecclesiastes 3:1 Holman CSB

I f you want to feel good about your life, then you'll need to do whatever it takes to feel good about the way that you spend your time. After all, how can you expect to build a healthy sense of self-worth if you're constantly goofing off—or if you're constantly wasting time doing things that get you nowhere?

By the way, the digital world can become a black hole for time, gobbling up every spare minute, keeping you up late at night, and robbing you of the chance to do more important stuff. Your job, and if you're smart, you'll choose to accept it, is to put the brakes on the Internet before the Internet puts the brakes on you.

As you decide how you'll spend the time that's allotted to you here on earth, remember that each new day is a special treasure to be savored and celebrated. As a Christian, you have much to celebrate and much to do. It's up to you, and you alone, to honor God for the gift of time by using that gift wisely.

As we surrender the use of our time
to the lordship of Christ, He will lead us to use it
in the most productive way imaginable.
Charles Stanley

Frustration is not the will of God.
There is time to do anything and everything
that God wants us to do.
Elisabeth Elliot

To choose time is to save time.
Francis Bacon

Social Networking Common Sense: Have an ironclad, non-negotiable time at night when you shut down your cell phone and your computer. Otherwise, you may find yourself staying up very late, goofing around, accomplishing almost nothing, and robbing yourself of much needed sleep.

Choosing to Behave Differently

Exercise your freedom by serving God, not by breaking rules.

I Peter 2:16 MSG

Okay, answer this question honestly: Do you behave differently because of your relationship with Jesus? Or do you behave in pretty much the same way that you would if you weren't a believer? Hopefully, the fact that you've invited Christ to reign over your heart means that you've made BIG changes in your thoughts, your actions, and your communications.

Doing the right thing is not always easy, especially when you're tired or frustrated. But, doing the wrong thing almost always leads to trouble (and, eventually, to poor self-esteem).

So if you want to feel good about yourself and your social network, don't follow the crowd—follow Jesus. And keep following Him every day of your life.

Although our actions have nothing to do with gaining our own salvation, they might be used by God to save somebody else! What we do really matters, and it can affect the eternities of people we care about.

Bill Hybels

Nobody is good by accident.
No man ever became holy by chance.

C. H. Spurgeon

Either God's Word keeps you from sin,
or sin keeps you from God's Word.

Corrie ten Boom

Social Networking Common Sense: If you're not sure that it's the right thing to do, don't do it! And if you're not sure that it's the right message to send, don't send it. You can't un-send messages that you've already sent, so be careful.

The Choice to Know Jesus

Then Jesus spoke to them again, saying,
"I am the light of the world. He who follows Me shall not
walk in darkness, but have the light of life."
John 8:12 NKJV

There's really no way around it: If you want to know God, you've got to get to know His Son. And that's good, because getting to know Jesus can—and should—be the most enriching experience of your life.

Can you honestly say that you're passionate about your faith and that you're really following Jesus? Hopefully so. But if you're preoccupied with other things—or if you're strictly a one-day-a-week Christian—then you're in need of a major-league spiritual makeover.

Jesus doesn't want you to be a lukewarm believer; Jesus wants you to be a "new creation" through Him. And that's exactly what you should want for yourself, too. Absolutely nothing is more important than your wholehearted commitment to your Creator and to His only begotten Son. Your faith must never be an afterthought; it must be your ultimate priority, your ultimate possession, and your ultimate passion. Everything else, including your social network, should come next. God should always come first.

Jesus is not a strong man making men and women
who gather around Him weak.
He is the Strong creating the strong.
E. Stanley Jones

Think of this—we may live together with Him
here and now, a daily walking with Him who loved us
and gave Himself for us.
Elisabeth Elliot

To walk out of His will is to walk into nowhere.
C. S. Lewis

Something to Think About: When Jesus endured His sacrifice on the cross, He paid a terrible price for you. What price are you willing to pay for Him?

Controlling Your Temper Online and Off

When you are angry, do not sin,
and be sure to stop being angry before the end of the day.
Do not give the devil a way to defeat you.
Ephesians 4:26–27 NCV

The high drama and constant flow of digital communications can sometimes get the better of us. Sooner or later, somebody says something we don't like, and we get angry. That's when we can allow minor Internet frustrations to cause us major real-life problems. If we respond by throwing an online temper tantrum, we're headed straight for trouble, and fast.

As the old saying goes, "Anger usually improves nothing but the arch of a cat's back." So don't allow feelings of anger or frustration to rule your digital life, or, for that matter, your real life—your life is simply too short for that, and you deserve much better treatment than that . . . from yourself.

When you strike out in anger,
you may miss the other person,
but you will always hit yourself.

Jim Gallery

Life is too short to spend it being
angry, bored, or dull.

Barbara Johnson

Anger unresolved will only bring you woe.

Kay Arthur

Something to Think About: When you lose your temper
. . . you lose.

Avoiding the Trap of Materialism

And He told them, "Watch out and be on guard against all greed, because one's life is not in the abundance of his possessions."

Luke 12:15 Holman CSB

The world focuses on stuff, but you shouldn't. And if your social network is overly concerned with the stuff that money can buy, it's time to start searching for a newer, smarter network.

On the stage of life, material possessions should play a rather small role. Of course, we all need the basic necessities like food, clothing, and a place to live. But once we've met those needs, the piling up of possessions creates more problems than it solves. Our real riches, of course, are not of this world. We're never really rich until we are rich in spirit.

Our society is in love with money and the things that money can buy. God is not. God cares about people, not possessions, and so must we. We must, to the best of our abilities, love our neighbors as ourselves, and we must, to the best of our abilities, resist the mighty temptation to place possessions ahead of people.

Money, in and of itself, is not evil; worshipping money is. So today, as you seek better ways to know your Creator, remember that God is almighty, but the dollar is not.

The cross is laid on every Christian.
It begins with the call to abandon
the attachments of this world.

Dietrich Bonhoeffer

Greed is enslaving.
The more you have, the more you want—
until eventually avarice consumes you.

Kay Arthur

Something to Think About: The world wants you to believe that "money and stuff" can buy happiness. Don't believe it! Genuine happiness comes not from money, but from the things that money can't buy—starting, of course, with your relationship to God and His only begotten Son.

You Need God's Word Every Day

For the word of God is living and effective and sharper than any two-edged sword, penetrating as far as to divide soul, spirit, joints, and marrow; it is a judge of the ideas and thoughts of the heart.

Hebrews 4:12 Holman CSB

Every day of your life, you need to take the time to shut down all those electrical gadgets and pick up the book God wrote. God's Word is unlike any other book. The words of Matthew 4:4 remind us that, "Man shall not live by bread alone but by every word that proceedeth out of the mouth of God" (KJV). As believers, we are instructed to study the Bible and meditate upon its meaning for our lives, yet far too many Bibles are laid aside by well-intentioned believers who would like to study the Bible if they could "just find the time."

Warren Wiersbe observed, "When the child of God looks into the Word of God, he sees the Son of God. And, he is transformed by the Spirit of God to share in the glory of God." God's Holy Word is, indeed, a transforming, life-changing, one-of-a-kind treasure. And it's up to you—and only you—to use it that way.

Faith is the virtue that enables us to believe
and obey the Word of God, for faith comes from hearing
and hearing from the Word of God.

Franklin Graham

Weave the unveiling fabric of God's word through
your heart and mind. It will hold strong,
even if the rest of life unravels.

Gigi Graham Tchividjian

Meditating upon His Word will inevitably bring peace of
mind, strength of purpose, and power for living.

Bill Bright

Something to Think About: If you have a choice to make, the Bible can help you make it. If you've got questions, the Bible has answers.

Avoiding the Media Hype

Let no one deceive himself. If anyone among you seems to be wise in this age, let him become a fool that he may become wise. For the wisdom of this world is foolishness with God. For it is written, "He catches the wise in their own craftiness."

I Corinthians 3:18–19 NKJV

Sometimes it's hard being a Christian, especially when the world keeps pumping out messages that are contrary to your faith.

The Internet and other forms of popular media are working around the clock in an attempt to rearrange your priorities. The media says that your appearance is all-important, that your clothes are all-important, that your car is all-important, and that partying is all-important. But guess what? Those messages are lies. The important things in your life have little to do with parties or appearances. The all-important things in life have to do with your faith, your family, and your future. Period.

Are you willing to stand up for your faith? If so, you'll be doing yourself a king-sized favor. And consider this: When you begin to speak up for God, isn't it logical to assume that you'll also begin to know Him in a more meaningful way?

So do yourself a favor: forget the media hype, and pay attention to God. Stand up for Him and be counted, not just in church where it's relatively easy to be a Christian, but also outside the church, where it's significantly harder. You owe it God . . . and you owe it to yourself.

Nothing speaks louder or more powerfully
than a life of integrity.

Charles Swindoll

The only ultimate disaster that can befall us,
I have come to realize,
is to feel ourselves to be home on earth.

Max Lucado

Social Networking Common Sense: The Internet is loaded with messages that are dangerous to your physical, emotional, and spiritual health. If you choose to believe those messages, you're setting yourself up for lots of trouble.

Plan Ahead

There is surely a future hope for you,
and your hope will not be cut off.

Proverbs 23:18 NIV

Maybe you've heard this old saying: "Look before you leap." Well, that saying may be old, but it still applies to you . . . especially on the Internet. Before you jump into something, you should look ahead and plan ahead. Otherwise, you might soon be sorry you jumped!

When you acquire the habit of planning ahead and thinking carefully before you do something, you'll usually make better choices. So when it comes to the important things in life, think ahead, make a plan, and stick to it. When you do, you'll think about the consequences of your actions before you do something silly . . . or dangerous . . . or both.

Allow your dreams a place in your prayers and plans. God-given dreams can help you move into the future He is preparing for you.

Barbara Johnson

Faith in God will not get for you everything you want, but it will get for you what God wants you to have. The unbeliever does not need what he wants; the Christian should want only what he needs.

Vance Havner

The only way you can experience abundant life is to surrender your plans to Him.

Charles Stanley

Something to Think About: The best time to decide how you're going to behave is before you find yourself in a difficult (or tempting) situation. So think ahead, plan ahead, and follow your plan!

The Choice to Experience Silence

Be still, and know that I am God.

Psalm 46:10 NKJV

The Bible teaches that a wonderful way to get to know God is simply to be still and listen to Him. But sometimes, you may find it hard to slow down and listen. After all, you live in a noisy world, a world loaded with constant communications, perpetual posts, massive amounts of text messages, and tons of Tweets. And as the demands of everyday life weigh down upon you, you may be tempted to ignore God's presence or—worse yet—to rebel against His teachings. But, when you quiet yourself and acknowledge His presence, God touches your heart and restores your spirits. So why not let Him do it right now? If you really want to know Him better, silence is a wonderful place to start.

Instead of waiting for the feeling, wait upon God.
You can do this by growing still and quiet, then expressing
in prayer what your mind knows is true about Him,
even if your heart doesn't feel it at this moment.

Shirley Dobson

True silence is the rest of the mind;
it is to the spirit what sleep is to the body,
nourishment and refreshment.

William Penn

I have come to recognize that He never asks us to do
anything He has not already done. He never takes us
anyplace where He has not been ahead of us.
What He is after is not performance,
but a relationship with us.

Gloria Gaither

Something to Think About: Want to talk to God? Then
don't make Him shout. If you really want to hear from God,
go to a quiet place and listen. If you keep listening long
enough and carefully enough, He'll start talking.

Better Choices Equal Better Self-Esteem

For it was You who created my inward parts;
You knit me together in my mother's womb. I will praise You,
because I have been remarkably and wonderfully made.

Psalm 139:13-14 Holman CSB

When you feel better about yourself, you make better choices. But sometimes, it's hard to feel good about yourself, especially when you live in a society that keeps sending out the message that you've got to be perfect.

Are you your own worst critic? And in response to that criticism, are you constantly trying to transform yourself into a person who meets society's expectations, but not God's expectations? If so, it's time to become a little more understanding of the person you see whenever you look into the mirror.

Millions of words have been written about various ways to improve self-esteem. Yet, maintaining a healthy self-image is, to a surprising extent, a matter of doing three things: 1. Obeying God 2. Thinking healthy thoughts 3. Finding things to do that please your Creator and yourself. When you concentrate on these things, your self-image will tend to take care of itself.

If you can forgive the person you were,
accept the person you are, and believe in the person you
will become, you are headed for joy.
So celebrate your life.
Barbara Johnson

Find satisfaction in him who made you,
and only then find satisfaction in yourself
as part of his creation.
St. Augustine

Something to Think About: When you learn to accept yourself, imperfections and all, you'll make better choices.

The Decision to Be Thankful

Praise the LORD. Give thanks to the LORD,
for he is good; his love endures forever.

Psalm 106:1 NIV

Because you're reading a book about social network-ing, it's a safe bet that you have the stuff that's required to be a member of a social network. You probably have access to at least one computer, and you probably have a cell phone, and lots more stuff, too. So here is today's question: are you thankful for all the stuff you have? Do you appreciate the life that you're privileged to live? You most certainly should be thankful. After all, when you stop to think about it, God has given you more blessings than you can count. So the question of the day is this: will you slow down long enough to thank your Heav-enly Father . . . or not?

Sometimes, life here on earth can be complicated, de-manding, and frustrating. When the demands of life leave you rushing from place to place with scarcely a moment to spare, you may fail to pause and thank your Creator for the countless blessings He has given you. Failing to thank God is understandable . . . but it's wrong. So here's something to remember: when it comes to knowing God, a thankful, humble heart isn't just helpful, it's essential.

God has promised that if we harvest well
with the tools of thanksgiving,
there will be seeds for planting in the spring.

Gloria Gaither

It is only with gratitude that life becomes rich.

Dietrich Bonhoeffer

Something to Think About: When is the best time to say "thanks" to God? Any Time. God never takes a vacation, and He's always ready to hear from you. So what are you waiting for?

Entrusting the Future to God

*"I say this because I know what I am planning for you,"
says the Lord. "I have good plans for you, not plans
to hurt you. I will give you hope and a good future."*
Jeremiah 29:11 NCV

As a member of the digital world, nobody has to tell you that the future is coming at you fast. And if you're a Christian, that's very good news indeed.

How bright is your future? Well, if you're a faithful believer, God's plans for you are so bright that you'd better wear shades. But here are some important follow-up questions: How bright do you believe your future to be? Are you expecting a terrific tomorrow, or are you dreading a terrible one? The answer you give will have a powerful impact on the way tomorrow turns out.

Do you trust in the ultimate goodness of God's plan for your life? Will you face tomorrow's challenges with optimism and hope? You should. After all, God created you for a very important reason: His reason. And you have important work to do: His work.

Today, as you live in the present and look to the future, remember that God has an amazing plan for you. Act—and believe—accordingly.

> We must trust as if it all depended on God
> and work as if it all depended on us.
>
> C. H.. Spurgeon

> Every man lives by faith, the nonbeliever as well as
> the saint; the one by faith in natural
> and the other by faith in God.
>
> A. W. Tozer

> Faith in faith is pointless.
> Faith in a living, active God moves mountains.
>
> Beth Moore

Something to Think About: Hope for the future isn't some pie-in-the-sky dream; hope for the future is simply one aspect of trusting God.

The Decision to Live Purposefully

I, therefore, the prisoner in the Lord, urge you to walk worthy of the calling you have received.

Ephesians 4:1 Holman CSB

Are you using your social network as a way to share your faith? Hopefully so, because sharing your faith is most certainly part of your purpose here on earth.

Life is best lived on purpose. And purpose, like everything else in the universe, begins with God. Whether you realize it or not, God has a plan for your life, a divine calling, a direction in which He is leading you. When you welcome God into your heart and establish a genuine relationship with Him, He will begin, in time, to make His purposes known.

Sometimes, God's intentions will be clear to you; other times, God's plan will seem uncertain at best. But even on those difficult days when you are unsure which way to turn, you must never lose sight of these overriding facts: God created you for a reason; He has important work for you to do; and He's waiting patiently for you to do it.

The really committed leave the safety of the harbor, accept the risk of the open seas of faith, and set their compasses for the place of total devotion to God and whatever life adventures He plans for them.

Bill Hybels

In the very place where God has put us, whatever its limitations, whatever kind of work it may be, we may indeed serve the Lord Christ.

Elisabeth Elliot

Something to Think About: Discovering God's purpose for your life requires a willingness to be open. God's plan is unfolding day by day. If you keep your eyes and your heart open, He'll reveal His plans. God has big things in store for you, but He may have quite a few lessons to teach you before you are fully prepared to do His will and fulfill His purposes.

Choosing to Have a Healthy Fear of God

Therefore, since we are receiving a kingdom that cannot be shaken, let us hold on to grace. By it, we may serve God acceptably, with reverence and awe.

Hebrews 12:28 Holman CSB

Whether you're online, or anywhere else for that matter, it pays to have a healthy respect for God. The Bible instructs us that a healthy fear of the Lord is the foundation of wisdom. Yet sometimes, in our shortsightedness, we fail to show respect for our Creator because we fail to obey Him. When we do, our disobedience always has consequences, and sometimes those consequences are severe.

When we honor the Father by obeying His commandments, we receive His love and His grace. Today, let us demonstrate our respect for God by developing a healthy fear of disobeying Him.

It is not possible that mortal men should be
thoroughly conscious of the divine presence
without being filled with awe.

C. H. Spurgeon

If we do not tremble before God,
the world's system seems wonderful to us
and pleasantly consumes us.

James Montgomery Boice

A healthy fear of God will do much
to deter us from sin.

Charles Swindoll

Social Networking Common Sense: When you're on the
Internet, you should be fearful of displeasing God. It's the
right kind of fear: Your respect for God should make you
fearful of disobeying Him . . . very fearful.

Choosing to Be Patient with Others and with Yourself

God has chosen you and made you his holy people.
He loves you. So always do these things:
Show mercy to others, be kind, humble, gentle, and patient.

Colossians 3:12 NCV

The digital world is full of people who are very impatient. Please don't be one of them.

The dictionary defines the word *patience* as "the ability to be calm, tolerant, and understanding." If that describes you, you can skip the rest of this page. But, if you're like most of us, you'd better keep reading.

For most of us, patience is a hard thing to master. Why? Because we have lots of things we want, and we want them NOW (if not sooner). But the Bible tells us that we must learn to wait patiently for the things that God has in store for us.

The next time you find your patience tested to the limit, remember that the world unfolds according to God's timetable, not yours. Sometimes, you must wait patiently, and that's as it should be. After all, think how patient God has been with you!

We must never think that patience is complacency.
Patience is endurance in action.

Warren Wiersbe

A keen sense of humor helps us to overlook
the unbecoming, understand the unconventional,
tolerate the unpleasant, overcome the unexpected,
and outlast the unbearable.

Billy Graham

Something to Think About: Want other people to be patient with you? Then you must do the same for them. Never expect other people to be more patient with you than you are with them.

The Decision to Worship God Every Day

Worship the Lord your God and . . . serve Him only.

Matthew 4:10 Holman CSB

Could you keep your network totally updated if you limited your social contacts to one hour a week? Probably not. So how can you expect to know God if you only spend an hour or two with Him each week? The answer is simple: If you really want to know God, you must be willing to spend time with Him every day. In other words, you must worship Him seven days a week, not just on Sundays.

God has a wonderful plan for your life, and an important part of that plan includes the time that you set aside for praise and worship. Every life, including yours, is based upon some form of worship. The question is not whether you will worship, but what you worship.

If you choose to worship God, you will receive a bountiful harvest of joy, peace, and abundance. But if you distance yourself from God by foolishly worshiping earthly possessions and personal gratification, you're making a huge mistake. So do this: Worship God today and every day. Worship Him with sincerity and thanksgiving. Write His name on your heart and rest assured that He, too, has written your name on His.

Worship is a voluntary act of gratitude offered
by the saved to the Savior, by the healed to the Healer,
by the delivered to the Deliverer.

Max Lucado

Worship is spiritual. Our worship must be more
than just outward expression,
it must also take place in our spirits.

Franklin Graham

Something to Think About: Worship is not meant to be boxed up in a church building on Sunday morning. To the contrary, praise and worship should be woven into the very fabric of your life.

Choosing Not to Worship the World

For the mind-set of the flesh is death,
but the mind-set of the Spirit is life and peace.

Romans 8:6 Holman CSB

We live in the real world, and we communicate in the digital world, but we must not worship either of these worlds. Our duty is to place God first and everything else second. But because we are fallible beings with imperfect faith, placing God in His rightful place is often difficult. In fact, at every turn, or so it seems, we are tempted to do otherwise.

The 21st-century world is a noisy, distracting place filled with countless opportunities to wander far from God's will. The world seems to cry, "Worship me with your time, your money, your energy, your time, and your thoughts!" But God commands otherwise: He commands us to worship Him and Him alone. Everything else, including (but certainly not limited to your social network) must be secondary.

Jesus calls you to be a non-conformist.
Live to be separated from the evils of the world.
Live to be different.

Billy Graham

The true Christian, though he is in revolt against
the world's efforts to brainwash him, is no mere rebel for
rebellion's sake. He dissents from the world because he
knows that it cannot make good on its promises.

A. W. Tozer

Something to Think About: Whose messages will you trust?
If you dwell on the world's messages, you're setting yourself
up for disaster. If you dwell on God's message, you're setting
yourself up for victory.

Choosing to Be Happy

I've learned by now to be quite content whatever my circumstances. I'm just as happy with little as with much, with much as with little. I've found the recipe for being happy whether full or hungry, hands full or hands empty.

Philippians 4:11-12 MSG

When will you celebrate God's marvelous creation: today or tomorrow? When will you make the choice to rejoice: now or later? When will you accept the happiness and peace that can (and should) be yours—in the present moment or in the distant future? The answer to these questions is straightforward: the best moment to accept God's gifts is the present one.

Happiness depends less upon our circumstances than upon our thoughts. When we turn our thoughts to God, to His gifts, and to His glorious creation, we experience the joy that God intends for His children. But, when we focus on the negative aspects of life, we inadvertently bring needless pain to our friends, to our families, and to ourselves.

Do you sincerely want to be a happy person? Then set your mind and your heart upon God's love and His grace. Seek a genuine, intimate, life-altering relationship with your Creator by studying His Word and trusting His promises. And while you're at it, count your blessings instead of your hardships. Then, after you've done these things, claim the joy, the peace, and the spiritual abundance that the Shepherd offers His sheep.

Happiness is the by-product of a life that is lived
in the will of God. When we humbly serve others,
walk in God's path of holiness, and do what He tells us,
then we will enjoy happiness.

Warren Wiersbe

No one is truly happy if he has what he wants,
but only if he wants something he should have.

St. Augustine

Social Networking Common Sense: Know the people in your social network. How? By making sure you really know who somebody is before you allow him to be on your friends list.

Choosing to Be Moderate

Be on your guard, so that your minds are not dulled from carousing, drunkenness, and worries of life.

Luke 21:34 Holman CSB

It's tempting to spend every spare moment kicking things around inside with your network of friends—but it's wrong. When it comes to your social network, you can certainly spend some time keeping things current, but you shouldn't spend all your time doing it. You need to be moderate.

Moderation and wisdom are traveling companions. If we are wise, we learn to control our appetites, our impulses, and our habits. When we do, we are blessed, in part, because God has created a world in which moderation is usually rewarded and overindulgence is usually punished.

No one can force you to be moderate, on the Internet or off. The decision to live moderately (and wisely) is yours and yours alone. And so are the consequences.

Virtue—even attempted virtue—brings light;
indulgence brings fog.

C. S. Lewis

Father, take our mistakes and turn them
into opportunities.

Max Lucado

To many, total abstinence is easier
than perfect moderation.

St. Augustine

Something to Think About: When in doubt, be moderate.
Moderation is wisdom in action.

Choosing to Encourage Others

But encourage each other daily,
while it is still called today,
so that none of you is hardened by sin's deception.

Hebrews 3:13 Holman CSB

While you're building your social network, be sure to build in lots of encouragement for all your friends. Why? Because life is a team sport, and all of us need occasional pats on the back from our teammates. As Christians, we are called upon to spread the Good News of Christ, and we are also called to spread a message of encouragement and hope to the world.

Whether you realize it or not, many people with whom you come in contact with every day are in desperate need of a smile or an encouraging word. The world can be a difficult place, and countless friends and family members may be troubled by the challenges of everyday life. Since you don't always know who needs your help, the best strategy is to try to encourage all the people who cross your path, whether you're on the Internet or anyplace else. So today, be a world-class source of encouragement to everyone you meet. Never has the need been greater.

A lot of people have gone further than they thought they could because someone else thought they could.

Zig Ziglar

No journey is complete that does not lead through some dark valleys. We can properly comfort others only with the comfort we ourselves have been given by God.

Vance Havner

God grant that we may not hinder those who are battling their way slowly into the light.

Oswald Chambers

Something to Think About: To find golden words, use the Golden Rule. When choosing the right words to say to someone else, think about the words that you would want to hear if you were standing in that person's shoes.

Choosing to Bear Witness to God's Truth

You will know the truth, and the truth will set you free.

John 8:32 Holman CSB

If you use your social network to share God's truth, you'll be blessed. After all, God is vitally concerned with truth. His Word teaches the truth; His Spirit reveals the truth; His Son leads us to the truth. When we open our hearts to God, and when we allow His Son to rule over our thoughts and our lives, God reveals Himself, and we come to understand the truth about ourselves and the Truth (with a capital T) about God's gift of grace.

The familiar words of John 8:32 remind us that when we come to know God's Truth, we are liberated. Have you been liberated by that Truth? And are you living in accordance with the eternal truths that you find in God's Holy Word? Hopefully so.

Today, as you fulfill the responsibilities that God has placed before you, ask yourself this question: "Do my thoughts and actions bear witness to the ultimate Truth that God has placed in my heart, or am I allowing the pressures of everyday life to overwhelm me?" It's a profound question that deserves an answer . . . now.

Let everything perish! Dismiss these empty vanities!
And let us take up the search for the truth.

St. Augustine

We must go out and live among them, manifesting
the gentle, loving spirit of our Lord.
We need to make friends before we can hope
to make converts.

Lottie Moon

Something to Think About: It's not enough to hear God's truth, or even to understand it. If you're serious about your faith, you must allow yourself to be transformed by God's truth. And then, you'll share God's truth.

Wisdom 101

Wisdom is the principal thing; therefore get wisdom.
And in all your getting, get understanding.

Proverbs 4:7 NKJV

Because you're probably a student, your head is undoubtedly filled with valuable information. But, there is much yet to learn. Wisdom is like a savings account: If you add to it consistently, then eventually you'll have a great sum. The secret to success is consistency.

Would you like to become wise? Then keep learning. Seek wisdom every day, and seek it in the right place. That place, of course, is not, first and foremost, the Internet. The first and best place to find wisdom is the Word of God. And remember this: it's not enough to simply read God's Word; you've also got to live by it.

Don't expect wisdom to come into your life like great chunks of rock on a conveyor belt. Wisdom comes privately from God as a by-product of right decisions, godly reactions, and the application of spiritual principles to daily circumstances.

Charles Swindoll

Wisdom is the right use of knowledge. To know is not to be wise. Many men know a great deal, and are all the greater fools for it. But to know how to use knowledge is to have wisdom.

C. H. Spurgeon

Something to Think About: Simply put, wisdom starts with God. If you don't have God's wisdom—and if you don't live according to God's rules—you'll pay a big price later.

The Choice to Be Courteous

Who is wise and understanding among you?
He should show his works by good conduct
with wisdom's gentleness.

James 3:13 Holman CSB

D oes the Bible instruct us in matters of online etiquette and courtesy? Of course it does. The words of Matthew 7:12 are clear: "In everything, therefore, treat people the same way you want them to treat you, for this is the Law and the Prophets" (NASB).

The Bible doesn't instruct, "In some things, treat people as you wish to be treated." And, it doesn't say, "From time to time, treat others with kindness." The Bible instructs us to treat others as we wish to be treated in every aspect of our daily lives.

Today try to be a little kinder than necessary to family members, friends, and total strangers. And as you consider all the things God has done for you, honor Him with your kind words and good deeds. He deserves no less, and neither do your loved ones.

Be so preoccupied with good will that you
haven't room for ill will.

E. Stanley Jones

Only the courteous can love,
but it is love that makes them courteous.

C. S. Lewis

Courtesy, like its opposite, is contagious.

Criswell Freeman

Something to Think About: Remember: courtesy isn't optional. If you disagree with somebody, do so without being disagreeable; if you're angry, hold your tongue; if you're frustrated or tired, don't argue . . . take a nap.

Meet with God Every Morning

Morning by morning he wakens me and opens my understanding to his will.
The Sovereign Lord has spoken to me, and I have listened.
Isaiah 50:4-5 NLT

Want to know God better? Then schedule a meeting with Him every day. And while you're at it, be sure to spend as much time focusing on God as you do focusing on your social contacts.

Daily life is a tapestry of habits, and no habit is more important to your spiritual health than the discipline of daily prayer and devotion to the Creator. When you begin each day with your head bowed and your heart lifted, you are reminded of God's love and God's laws.

Each day has 1,440 minutes—do you value your relationship with God enough to spend a few of those minutes with Him? He deserves that much of your time and more. But if you find that you're simply "too busy" for a daily chat with your Father in heaven, it's time to take a long, hard look at your priorities and your values.

A person with no devotional life generally struggles with faith and obedience.

Charles Stanley

Maintenance of the devotional mood is indispensable to success in the Christian life.

A. W. Tozer

Jesus challenges you and me to keep our focus daily on the cross of His will if we want to be His disciples.

Anne Graham Lotz

Something to Think About: Get reacquainted with God every day: You should stay much closer to God than to anybody (or, for that matter, everybody) in your social network.

Saying No to Immorality

Therefore, brothers, by the mercies of God, I urge you to present your bodies as a living sacrifice, holy and pleasing to God; this is your spiritual worship.

Romans 12:1 Holman CSB

It's tempting to visit bad sites, do bad things, and look at sordid stuff on the Internet. But you've got to be strong enough to say no to these temptations. And there's a lot riding on your decision to do the right things.

The temptations of the world sit atop a slippery slope. If you sample those temptations even once, you're on that slope. Perhaps, if you're lucky, you can keep your footing. Perhaps not. But of this you can be certain: if you never step foot on the slippery slope of sin, you'll never slide off.

You live in a world that encourages you to "try" any number of things which are dangerous to your spiritual, mental, or physical health. It's a world brimming with traps and temptations designed to corrupt your character and wreck your life. Please don't fall into those traps.

A pure theology and a loose morality will never mix.

C. H. Spurgeon

You should not believe your conscience and
your feelings more than the word which the Lord who
receives sinners preaches to you.

Martin Luther

Morality and immorality are not defined by man's
changing attitudes and social customs.
They are determined by the God of the universe, whose
timeless standards cannot be ignored with impunity.

James Dobson

Something to Think About: If you are a Christian, your
hero (and the One you should seek to imitate) is Christ.
So follow in His footsteps and obey His commandments.
When you do, you'll be secure.

The Choice to Get Involved in a Church

For we are God's fellow workers; you are God's field,
you are God's building.

I Corinthians 3:9 NKJV

Hopefully, your social network taps into your local church. In the Book of Acts, Luke reminds us to "feed the church of God" (20:28). As Christians who have been saved by a loving, compassionate Creator, we are compelled not only to worship Him in our hearts but also to worship Him in the presence of fellow believers.

Do you attend church regularly? And when you attend, are you an active participant, or are you just taking up space? The answer to these questions will have a profound impact on the quality and direction of your spiritual journey. So do yourself a favor: become actively involved in your church. Don't just go to church out of habit. Go to church out of a sincere desire to know and worship God. When you do, you'll be blessed by the One who sent His Son to die so that you might have everlasting life.

The Bible knows nothing of solitary religion.

John Wesley

How beautiful it is to learn that grace isn't fragile,
and that in the family of God we can fail
and not be a failure.

Gloria Gaither

It has always been the work of the church to bring others
to belief in Christ and to experience
a personal relationship with Him.

Charles Stanley

Something to Think About: Make church a celebration,
not an obligation: Your attitude toward church is important, in part, because it is contagious . . . so celebrate accordingly!

The Marathon

Thanks be to God! He gives us the victory through our Lord
Jesus Christ. Therefore, my dear brothers, stand firm.
Let nothing move you. Always give yourselves fully to
the work of the Lord, because you know that your labor
in the Lord is not in vain.

I Corinthians 15:57-58 NIV

D o you sincerely want to live a life that is pleasing
to God? If so, you must remember that life is not
a sprint, it's a marathon that calls for preparation,
determination, and lots of perseverance.

Are you one of those people who doesn't give up easily, or are you quick to bail out when the going gets tough?
If you've developed the unfortunate habit of giving up at
the first sign of trouble, it's probably time for you to have a
heart-to-heart talk with the person you see every time you
look in the mirror.

Jesus finished what He began, and so should you. Despite His suffering, despite the shame of the cross, Jesus was
steadfast in His faithfulness to God. You, too, must remain
faithful, especially when times are tough.

Do you want to build a closer relationship with God? Then don't give up. And if you're facing a difficult situation, remember this: whatever your problem, God can handle it. Your job is to keep persevering until He does.

Perseverance is more than endurance.
It is endurance combined with absolute assurance and certainty that what we are looking for is going to happen.
Oswald Chambers

We are all on our way somewhere.
We'll get there if we just keep going.
Barbara Johnson

Failure is one of life's most powerful teachers.
How we handle our failures determines whether we're going to simply "get by" in life or "press on."
Beth Moore

Social Networking Common Sense: If you value your privacy (and you should), keep your passwords private.

Choosing to Talk Things Over with God

If you don't know what you're doing, pray to the Father. He loves to help. You'll get his help, and won't be condescended to when you ask for it. Ask boldly, believingly, without a second thought. People who "worry their prayers" are like wind-whipped waves. Don't think you're going to get anything from the Master that way, adrift at sea, keeping all your options open.

James 1:5-8 MSG

Okay, let's say you're about to make a big decision. Whom should you turn to? Friends? Online chat rooms? Self-help gurus? Well, the first place you should turn is to your Father in heaven. If you talk to God sincerely and often, He won't lead you astray. Instead, God will guide you and help you make more intelligent choices . . . if you take the time to talk with Him.

If you have questions about whether you should do something or not, pray about it. If there is something you're worried about, ask God to comfort you. If you're having trouble with your relationships, ask God to help you sort things out. As you pray more, you'll discover that God is always near and that He's always ready to hear from you. So don't worry about things; pray about them. God is waiting . . . and listening!

Prayer is the same as the breathing of air for the lungs.
Exhaling makes us get rid of our dirty air.
Inhaling gives clean air. To exhale is to confess,
to inhale is to be filled with the Holy Spirit.

Corrie ten Boom

Prayer accomplishes more than anything else.

Bill Bright

Something to Think About: When you have questions you can't answer, you can talk things over with friends. But don't forget to talk things over with God because prayer answers lots of questions.

Choosing to Seek Strength from God

The Lord is my strength and my song;
He has become my salvation.

Exodus 15:2 Holman CSB

Where do you go to find strength? The gym? The health food store? The espresso bar? There's a better source of strength, of course, and that source is God. He is a never-ending source of strength and courage if you call upon Him.

Have you "tapped in" to the power of God? Have you turned your life and your heart over to Him, or are you muddling along under your own power? The answer to this question will determine the quality of your life here on earth and the destiny of your life throughout all eternity. So start tapping in—and remember that when it comes to strength, God is the Ultimate Source.

Our Lord never drew power from Himself,
He drew it always from His Father.

Oswald Chambers

And in truth, if we only knew it, our chief fitness is our
utter helplessness. His strength is made perfect,
not in our strength, but in our weakness.
Our strength is only a hindrance.

Hannah Whitall Smith

By ourselves we are not capable of suffering bravely,
but the Lord possesses all the strength we lack and will
demonstrate His power when we undergo persecution.

Corrie ten Boom

Something to Think About: If you're energy is low or your
nerves are frazzled, perhaps you need to slow down and
have a heart-to-heart talk with God. And while you're at
it, remember that God is bigger than your problems . . .
much bigger.

Getting Smarter Day by Day

When I was a child, I spoke and thought and reasoned as a child does. But when I grew up, I put away childish things.

I Corinthians 13:11 NLT

Are you a fully-grown person? Physically: maybe so. But spiritually? No way! And thank goodness that you're not! Even if you're very mature for your age, you've still got lots of room to grow.

The 19th-century writer Hannah Whitall Smith observed, "The maturity of a Christian experience cannot be reached in a moment." No kidding. In truth, the search for spiritual growth lasts a lifetime.

When we cease to grow, either emotionally or spiritually, we do ourselves and our families a profound disservice. But, if we study God's Word, if we obey His commandments, and if we live in the center of His will, we will not be "stagnant" believers; we will, instead, be growing Christians . . . and that's exactly what God wants for our lives. Come to think of it, that's exactly what you should want, too.

When it comes to walking with God, there is no such thing as instant maturity. God doesn't mass produce His saints. He hand tools each one, and it always takes longer than we expected.

Charles Swindoll

I'm not what I want to be. I'm not what I'm going to be. But, thank God, I'm not what I was!

Gloria Gaither

Being a Christian means accepting the terms of creation, accepting God as our maker and redeemer, and growing day by day into an increasingly glorious creature in Christ, developing joy, experiencing love, maturing in peace.

Eugene Peterson

Something to Think About: Whether you're on the Internet or anywhere else, being mature means that you consistently make wise choices. Being immature means that you consistently make unwise choices. It's as simple as that.

Choosing to Serve

*If they serve Him obediently, they will end their days in
prosperity and their years in happiness.*

Job 36:11 Holman CSB

If you genuinely want to make your social network a
force for good in this world, you must ask yourself this
question: "How does God want me and my friends to
serve others?"

Whatever your age, wherever you happen to be, you
may be certain of this: service to others is an integral part
of God's plan for your life.

Are you willing to become a humble servant for Christ?
Are you willing to pitch in and make the world a better
place, or are you determined to keep all your blessings to
yourself. The answers to these questions will determine the
quantity and the quality of the service you render to God
and to His children.

Today, you may feel the temptation to take more than
you give. You may be tempted to withhold your generosity.
Or you may be tempted to build yourself up in the eyes of
your friends. Resist those temptations. Instead, serve your
friends quietly and without fanfare. Find a need and fill it

. . . humbly. Lend a helping hand . . . anonymously. Share a word of kindness . . . with quiet sincerity. As you go about your daily activities, remember that the Savior of all humanity made Himself a servant, and we, as His followers, must do no less.

Service is the pathway to real significance.
Rick Warren

Doing something positive toward another person is a practical approach to feeling good about yourself.
Barbara Johnson

Through our service to others,
God wants to influence our world for Him.
Vonette Bright

Something to Think About: If you choose to serve, you'll be doing the world (and yourself) a big favor.

Choosing to Be a Good Example

We have around us many people whose lives tell us what faith means. So let us run the race that is before us and never give up. We should remove from our lives anything that would get in the way and the sin that so easily holds us back.

Hebrews 12:1 NCV

Whether you're posting on the Internet, texting to a friend, or talking to people face-to-face, how can other people tell you're a Christian? Well, you can tell them, of course. And make no mistake about it: talking about your faith in God is a very good thing to do. But simply telling people about Jesus isn't enough. You must also be willing to show people how an extremely devoted Christian (like you) should behave.

Does your social network reflect your values? Is your life a picture book of your creed? Do your actions line up with your beliefs? And are you willing to practice the philosophy that you preach? If so, congratulations. If not, it's time for a change.

Like it or not, your behavior is a powerful example to others. The question is not whether you will be an example to your family and friends; the question is what kind of example will you be.

Corrie ten Boom advised, "Don't worry about what you do not understand. Worry about what you do understand in the Bible but do not live by." And that's sound advice because your family and friends are always watching . . . and so, for that matter, is God.

Our walk counts far more than our talk, always!
George Mueller

Something to Think About: You can choose to be a good example . . . or not. The choice you make will have a big impact on your own life and on the lives of others, so choose carefully.

When You Make Mistakes

The one who conceals his sins will not prosper,
but whoever confesses and renounces them will find mercy.
Proverbs 28:13 Holman CSB

Mistakes: nobody likes 'em but everybody makes 'em. Sometimes, even if you're a very good person, you're going to mess things up. And when you do, God is always ready to forgive you—He'll do His part, but you should be willing to do your part, too. Here's what you need to do:

1. If you've been engaging in behavior that is against the will of God, cease and desist (that means stop). 2. If you made a mistake, learn from it and don't repeat it (that's called getting smarter). 3. If you've hurt somebody, apologize and ask for forgiveness (that's called doing the right thing). 4. Ask for God's forgiveness, too (He'll give it whenever you ask, but you do need to ask!).

Have you made a mistake? If so, today is the perfect day to make things right with everybody (and the word "everybody" includes yourself, your family, your friends, and your God).

Mistakes are the price you pay for being human; repeated mistakes are the price you pay for being stubborn. So don't be hardheaded: learn from your experiences—the first time!

Father, take our mistakes and turn them into opportunities.
Max Lucado

God is able to take mistakes,
when they are committed to Him, and make of them something for our good and for His glory.
Ruth Bell Graham

Something to Think About: Mistakes happen in the digital world and in the real world. When you make a mistake (and you will) the best time to fix those mistakes is now, not later.

When You're Online (or Anyplace Else) Don't Betray Your Conscience

For indeed, the kingdom of God is within you.

Luke 17:21 NKJV

It has been said that character is what we are when nobody is watching. How true. When we do things that we know to be wrong—or when we say things that we know to be untrue—we may fool some of the people some of the time. But even then, God is watching . . . and we can never conceal our actions from Him.

Few things in life torment us more than a guilty conscience. And, few things in life provide more contentment than the knowledge that we are obeying the conscience that God has placed in our hearts.

So here's a simple (but powerful) tip: never forsake your conscience. And remember this: when you walk with God, your character will take care of itself . . . and you won't need to look over your shoulder to see who, besides God, is watching.

The convicting work of the Holy Spirit awakens,
disturbs, and judges.

Franklin Graham

Every secret act of character, conviction,
and courage has been observed in living color
by our omniscient God.

Bill Hybels

A good conscience is a continual feast.

Francis Bacon

Social Networking Common Sense: When you're posting information or texting stuff to a friend, listen to your conscience. If you listen to your conscience, you'll make better choices. If you don't, you won't.

Choosing to Forgive

Be even-tempered, content with second place,
quick to forgive an offense. Forgive as quickly and completely
as the Master forgave you. And regardless of what else you
put on, wear love. It's your basic, all-purpose garment.
Never be without it.

Colossians 3:13-14 MSG

Okay, somebody has done something to make you mad. So should you mobilize your entire social network to attack the guilty party using whatever dirty laundry you can find? Well, not exactly. If you're a Christian, you're commanded (as in "that's an order!") to forgive the other guy every time.

Are you the kind of guy or girl who has a tough time forgiving and forgetting? If so, welcome to the club. Most of us find it difficult to forgive the people who have hurt us. And that's too bad because life would be much simpler if we could forgive people "once and for all" and be done with it. Yet forgiveness is seldom that easy. Usually, the decision to forgive is straightforward, but the process of forgiving is more difficult. Forgiveness is a journey that requires effort, time, perseverance, and prayer.

If there exists even one person whom you have not forgiven (and that includes yourself), obey God's commandment: forgive that person today. And remember that bitterness, anger, and regret are not part of God's plan for your life. Forgiveness is.

If you sincerely wish to forgive someone, pray for that person. And then pray for yourself by asking God to heal your heart. Don't expect forgiveness to be easy or quick, but rest assured: with God as your partner, you can forgive . . . and you will.

We are products of our past,
but we don't have to be prisoners of it.
God specializes in giving people a fresh start.
Rick Warren

Something to Think About: Holding a grudge? Drop it. Never expect other people to be more forgiving than you are. And remember: the best time to forgive is now.

Open Your Heart to God

*And we know that in all things God works
for the good of those who love him, who have been
called according to his purpose.*

Romans 8:28 NIV

When you stop to think about it, your social network is designed to help you get to know other people. But are you just as interested in getting to know God? Hopefully so.

If you want to know God in a more meaningful way, you'll need to open up your heart and let Him in. C. S. Lewis observed, "A person's spiritual health is exactly proportional to his love for God." If you hope to receive a full measure of God's spiritual blessings, you must invite your Creator to rule over your heart. When you honor God in this way, His love expands to fill your heart and bless your life.

St. Augustine wrote, "I love you, Lord, not doubtingly, but with absolute certainty. Your Word beat upon my heart until I fell in love with you, and now the universe and everything in it tells me to love you."

Today, open your heart to the Father. And let your obedience be a fitting response to His never-ending love.

If you want to know the will and voice of God,
you must give the time and effort to cultivate
a love relationship with Him. That is what He wants!

Henry Blackaby

Man was created by God to know and love Him in
a permanent, personal relationship.

Anne Graham Lotz

The truth of the Gospel is intended to free us to
love God and others with our whole heart.

John Eldredge

Something to Think About: When you sincerely open your
heart to God, you will find it easier to obey Him.

Working Diligently

*Don't work only while being watched, in order to please men,
but as slaves of Christ, do God's will from your heart. Render
service with a good attitude, as to the Lord and not to men.*

Ephesians 6:6-7 Holman CSB

Social networking is the sort of thing you do in your
spare time. So how does God want to spend the rest
of your time? Well the Bible makes it clear: God
wants you to work diligently. That's why He doesn't reward
mediocrity. Instead, God has created a world in which hard
work is rewarded and sloppy work is not. Sure, we may seek
ease over excellence, or we may be tempted to take short-
cuts. But God intends that we walk the straight and narrow
path.

Today, listen to God's Word by doing good work.
Wherever you find yourself, whatever your job description,
do your work, and do it with all your heart. When you do,
you will most certainly win the recognition of your peers.
But more importantly, God will bless your efforts and use
you in ways that only He can understand. So do your work
with focus and dedication. And leave the rest up to God.

You can't climb the ladder of life
with your hands in your pockets.

Barbara Johnson

God does not dispense strength and encouragement
like a druggist fills your prescription.
The Lord doesn't promise to give us something to take
so we can handle our weary moments. He promises us
Himself. That is all. And that is enough.

Charles Swindoll

Great relief and satisfaction can come from seeking
God's priorities for us in each season,
discerning what is "best" in the midst of many noble
opportunities, and pouring our most
excellent energies into those things.

Beth Moore

Something to Think About: Whether you realize it or not,
your work always speaks for itself: So make sure that your
work speaks well of your efforts.

Don't Overestimate the Importance of Appearances

As the water reflects the face, so the heart reflects the person.

Proverbs 27:19 Holman CSB

Sure you want to look good on Facebook and MySpace. But please don't become too concerned about looking too good. The world sees you as you appear to be; God sees you as you really are. He sees your heart, and He understands your intentions. The opinions of others should be relatively unimportant to you; however, God's view of you—His understanding of your actions, your thoughts, and your motivations—should be vitally important.

Few things in life are more futile than "keeping up appearances" in order to impress your friends and your dates— yet the media would have you believe otherwise. The media would have you believe that everything depends on the color of your hair, the condition of your wardrobe, and the model of the car you drive. But nothing could be further from the truth. What is important, of course, is pleasing your Father in heaven. You please Him when your intentions are pure and your actions are just. When you do, you will be blessed today, tomorrow, and forever.

Outside appearances, things like the clothes you wear or the car you drive, are important to other people but totally unimportant to God. Trust God.

Marie T. Freeman

It is comfortable to know that we are responsible to God and not to man. It is a small matter to be judged of man's judgement.

Lottie Moon

Something to Think About: When making judgments about your friends, don't focus on appearances. Focus on values.

Be Humble

*Humble yourselves, therefore, under God's mighty hand,
that he may lift you up in due time.*

I Peter 5:6 NIV

Is your Facebook page designed to make you look like the coolest thing since the invention of ice? Or the hottest thing since the invention of fire? Hopefully not. Why? Because God wants you to be more humble than that.

Face it: on the road to spiritual growth, pride is a massive roadblock. The more prideful you are, the more difficult it is to know God. When you experience success, it's easy to puff out your chest and proclaim, "I did that!" But it's wrong. Dietrich Bonhoeffer was correct when he observed, "It is very easy to overestimate the importance of our own achievements in comparison with what we owe others." In other words, reality breeds humility. So if you want to know God better, be humble. Otherwise, you'll be building a roadblock between you and your Creator (and that's a very bad thing to do!).

Do you wish to rise? Begin by descending.
You plan a tower that will pierce the clouds?
Lay first the foundation of humility.

St. Augustine

The great characteristic of the saint is humility.

Oswald Chambers

Nothing sets a person so much out of
the devil's reach as humility.

Jonathan Edwards

Something to Think About: Do you value humility above
status? If so, God will smile upon you. But if you value status above humility, you're inviting God's displeasure. In
short, humility pleases God; pride does not.

The Decision to Guard Your Heart and Mind

Summing it all up, friends, I'd say you'll do best by filling your minds and meditating on things true, noble, reputable, authentic, compelling, gracious, the best, not the worst; the beautiful, not the ugly; things to praise, not things to curse. Put into practice what you learned from me, what you heard and saw and realized. Do that, and God, who makes everything work together, will work you into his most excellent harmonies.

Philippians 4:8-9 MSG

It's easy to get lost on the Internet, and it's easy to compromise your values. But God wants to keep you safe, and that's exactly what He'll do if you let Him.

You are near and dear to God. He loves you more than you can imagine, and He wants the very best for you. And one more thing: God wants you to guard your heart.

Every day, you are faced with choices . . . lots of them. You can do the right thing, or not. You can tell the truth, or not. You can be kind, and generous, and obedient. Or not.

Today, the world will offer you countless opportunities to let down your guard and, by doing so, let the devil do his worst. So be watchful and obedient. Guard your heart by giving it to your Heavenly Father. It is safe with Him.

There may be no trumpet sound or loud applause
when we make a right decision,
just a calm sense of resolution and peace.

Gloria Gaither

Prayer guards hearts and minds and causes
God to bring peace out of chaos.

Beth Moore

Something to Think About: If you're not sure what Internet site to visit, or what kind of text to sent to a friend, slow down and listen to your conscience. That little voice inside your head is remarkably dependable, but you can't depend upon it if you never listen to it. So stop, listen, and learn—your conscience is almost always right!

Avoid the Constant Critics

*Therefore encourage one another
and build each other up as you are already doing.*
I Thessalonians 5:11 Holman CSB

A re you determined to make your little corner of the digital world a gossip-free zone, a place that encourages everybody to feel better about themselves. Hopefully so. And while you're at it, steer clear of the ceaseless critics and the chronic fault-finders.

In the book of James, we are issued a clear warning: "Don't criticize one another, brothers" (4:11 Holman CSB). Undoubtedly, James understood the paralyzing power of chronic negativity, and so should you.

Negativity is highly contagious, and can be highly hazardous to your sense of self-worth. So do yourself a major-league favor: find friends who make you feel better about yourself, not worse. Make no mistake: You deserve friends like that . . . and they deserve to have an encouraging friend like you.

A keen sense of humor helps us to overlook
the unbecoming, understand the unconventional,
tolerate the unpleasant, overcome the unexpected,
and outlast the unbearable.

Billy Graham

Never be afraid of the world's censure;
it's praise is much more to be dreaded.

C. H. Spurgeon

The scrutiny we give other people
should be for ourselves.

Oswald Chambers

Something to Think About: If you're tempted to be criti-
cal of others, remember that your ability to judge others
requires a level of insight that you simply don't have. So do
everybody (including yourself) a favor: don't criticize.

Choosing Integrity

A good name is to be chosen over great wealth.
Proverbs 22:1 Holman CSB

Hey, would you like a time-tested, ironclad formula for success? Here it is: guard your integrity like you guard your wallet.

It has been said on many occasions and in many ways that honesty is the best policy. For Christians, it is far more important to note that honesty is God's policy. And if we are to be servants worthy of our Savior, Jesus Christ, we must be honest, forthright, and trustworthy.

Telling the truth means telling the whole truth. And that means summoning the courage to deliver bad news when necessary. And for some of us, especially those of us who are card-carrying people pleasers, telling the whole truth can be difficult indeed (especially if we're pretty sure that the truth will make somebody mad). Still, if we wish to fashion successful lives, we've got to learn to be totally truthful—part-time truth-telling doesn't cut the mustard.

Sometimes, honesty is difficult; sometimes, honesty is painful; sometimes, honesty is inconvenient; but honesty is always God's way. In the Book of Proverbs, we read, "The

Lord detests lying lips, but he delights in men who are truthful" (12:22 NIV). Clearly, truth is God's way, and it must be our way, too, even when telling the truth is difficult.

God never called us to naïveté. He called us to integrity . . . . The biblical concept of integrity emphasizes mature innocence not childlike ignorance.

Beth Moore

Integrity is the glue that holds our way of life together. We must constantly strive to keep our integrity intact. When wealth is lost, nothing is lost; when health is lost, something is lost; when character is lost, all is lost.

Billy Graham

Social Networking Common Sense: Whether you're online or anywhere else, be quick to remove yourself from situations that might cause you to compromise your integrity.

Focusing on Spiritual Matters

*For those whose lives are according to the flesh think about
the things of the flesh, but those whose lives are according
to the Spirit, about the things of the Spirit.*

Romans 8:5 Holman CSB

It's easy to focus on your social network. After all, it's
right there on your computer screen, or it keeps pop-
ping up on your cell phone. But to focus completely on
things digital is a dead end. You're far better off to focus on
things spiritual.

Is Christ the focus of your life? Are you fired with enthusiasm for Him? Are you an energized Christian who al-
lows God's Son to reign over every aspect of your day? Make
no mistake: that's exactly what God intends for you to do.

God has given you the gift of eternal life through His
Son. In response to God's priceless gift, you are instructed
to focus your thoughts, your prayers, and your energies upon
God and His only begotten Son. To do so, you must resist
the subtle yet powerful temptation to become a "spiritual
dabbler."

A person who dabbles in the Christian faith is unwilling to place God in His rightful place: above all other things. Resist that temptation; make God the cornerstone and the touchstone of your life. When you do, He will give you all the strength and wisdom you need to live victoriously for Him.

Think of this—we may live together with Him
here and now, a daily walking with Him who loved us
and gave Himself for us.

Elisabeth Elliot

Paul did one thing. Most of us dabble in forty things.
Are you a doer or a dabbler?

Vance Havner

Something to Think About: How much time do you spend focusing on God and His will for your life? If you answered, "Not much," it's time to turn off your computer and reorder your priorities.

First Things First

Therefore, get your minds ready for action,
being self-disciplined . . . .

1 Peter 1:13 Holman CSB

"First things first." These words are easy to speak but hard to put into practice. For busy guys and girls living in a highly digitized—and demanding—world, placing first things first can be difficult indeed. Why? Because so many people are expecting so many things from us!

If you're having trouble prioritizing your day, perhaps you've been trying to organize your life according to your own plans, not God's. A better strategy, of course, is to take your daily obligations and place them in the hands of the One who created you. To do so, you must prioritize your day according to God's commandments, and you must seek His will and His wisdom in all matters. Then, you can face the day with the assurance that the same God who created our universe out of nothingness will help you place first things first in your own life.

Do you feel overwhelmed or confused? Turn the concerns of this day over to God—prayerfully, earnestly, and often. Then, listen for His answer . . . and trust the answer He gives.

He is no fool who gives what he cannot
keep to gain what he cannot lose.

Jim Elliot

Not now becomes never.

Martin Luther

I've found that the worst thing I can do when it
comes to any kind of potential pressure situation
is to put off dealing with it.

John Maxwell

Something to Think About: Decide how much of your time God deserves, and then give it to Him. Don't organize your day so that God gets "what's left." Give Him what you honestly believe He deserves.

Sharing Your Testimony

This and this only has been my appointed work: getting this news to those who have never heard of God, and explaining how it works by simple faith and plain truth.

I Timothy 2:7 MSG

A good way to build your faith is by talking about it—and that's precisely what God wants you to do. Whether you're operating in the digital realm or talking to somebody fact-to-face, your testimony is important.

In his second letter to Timothy, Paul shares a message to believers of every generation when he writes, "God has not given us a spirit of timidity" (1:7). Paul's meaning is clear: When sharing your faith, you must be courageous and unashamed.

Let's face facts: You live in a world that desperately needs the healing message of Jesus Christ. Every believer, including you, bears responsibility for sharing the Good News. And it is important to remember that you give your testimony through your words and your actions.

So today, preach the Gospel through your words and your deeds . . . and keep preaching it for the rest of your life.

If we are ever going to be or do anything for our Lord,
now is the time.

Vance Havner

One of the best ways to witness to family, friends,
and neighbors is to let them see the difference
Jesus has made in your life.

Anne Graham Lotz

There is nothing anybody else can do that can
stop God from using us.
We can turn everything into a testimony.

Corrie ten Boom

Something to Think About: D. L. Moody, the famed evangelist from Chicago, said, "Remember, a small light will do a great deal when it is in a very dark place. Put one little tallow candle in the middle of a large hall, and it will give a great deal of light." Make certain that your candle is always lit. Give your testimony, and trust God to do the rest.

The Choice to Be a Courageous Christian

Be strong and courageous, and do the work.
Don't be afraid or discouraged, for the Lord God,
my God, is with you. He won't leave you or forsake you.

I Chronicles 28:20 Holman CSB

Every person's life is a tapestry of events: some wonderful, some not-so-wonderful, and some downright disastrous. When we visit the mountaintops of life, praising God isn't hard—in fact, it's easy. In our moments of triumph, we can bow our heads and thank God for our victories. But when we fail to reach the mountaintops, when we endure the inevitable losses that are a part of every person's life, we find it much tougher to give God the praise He deserves. Yet wherever we find ourselves, whether on the mountaintops of life or in life's darkest valleys, we must still offer thanks to God, giving thanks in all circumstances.

When you form a genuine one-on-one relationship with God, you can be comforted by the fact that wherever you find yourself, whether at the top of the mountain or the depths of the valley, God is there with you. And because your Creator cares for you and protects you, you can live courageously.

Choose Jesus Christ! Deny yourself, take up the Cross, and follow Him—for the world must be shown. The world must see, in us, a discernible, visible, startling difference.

Elisabeth Elliot

The fear of God is the death of every other fear.

C. H. Spurgeon

Something to Think About: With God as your partner, you have nothing to fear. Why? Because you and God, working together, can handle absolutely anything that comes your way. So the next time you'd like an extra measure of courage, recommit yourself to a true one-on-one relationship with your Creator. When you sincerely turn to Him, He will never fail you.

Deciding Not to Be Judgmental

Stop judging others, and you will not be judged.
Stop criticizing others, or it will all come back on you.
If you forgive others, you will be forgiven.

Luke 6:37 NLT

I t's easy to judge others, especially when you don't have to face them in person. That's one reason that the Internet is filled with harsh criticisms of other people. It's easy to pass on a negative comment about somebody you don't like, but it's wrong.

Here's something worth thinking about: If you judge other people harshly, God will judge you in the same fashion. But that's not all (thank goodness!). The Bible also promises that if you forgive others, you, too, will be forgiven.

Have you developed the bad habit of behaving yourself like an amateur judge and jury, assigning blame and condemnation wherever you go? If so, it's time to grow up and obey God. When it comes to judging everything and everybody, God doesn't need your help . . . and He doesn't want it.

Christians think they are prosecuting attorneys
or judges, when, in reality, God has called
all of us to be witnesses.

Warren Wiersbe

It is time that the followers of Jesus revise
their language and learn to speak respectfully
of non-Christian peoples.

Lottie Moon

Jesus lives in the community;
He only visits the church.

Anonymous

Something to Think About: Your ability to judge others
requires a divine insight that you simply don't have. So do
everybody (including yourself) a favor: don't judge.

Learning When to Say No

If you're not welcomed, not listened to,
quietly withdraw. Don't make a scene.
Shrug your shoulders and be on your way.

Mark 6:11 MSG

Sometimes, you may feel pressured to compromise yourself, and you may be afraid of what will happen if you firmly say no. You may be afraid that you'll be rejected. But here's a tip: don't worry too much about rejection, especially when you're rejected for doing the right thing.

Pleasing other people is a good thing . . . up to a point. But you must never allow your "willingness to please" to interfere with your own good judgment or with God's commandments.

Instead of being afraid of rejection, focus on pleasing your Creator first and always. Whether you're chatting online or talking to someone face-to-face, never be afraid to stand up for what you believe. And when it comes to the world and all its inhabitants, don't worry too much about the folks you can't please. Focus, instead, on doing the right thing—and leave the rest up to God

Too many Christians have geared their program to please,
to entertain, and to gain favor from this world.
We are concerned with how much, instead of how little,
like this age we can become.

Billy Graham

Those who, to please their listeners, avoid giving
a forthright declaration of the will of God
become slaves of those they would please
and abandon the service of God.

Basil the Great

You must never sacrifice your relationship with God for
the sake of a relationship with another person.

Charles Stanley

Social Networking Common Sense: Don't ever give personal information, over the Internet or otherwise, to someone you don't know. No exceptions. Even if a very nice-sounding person asks for that information, say no.

Too Busy?

Be careful not to forget the Lord.

Deuteronomy 6:12 Holman CSB

It takes time to cultivate and maintain a good social network . . . lots of time. So if you're busy building your connections, you'll have less time for other things. And you may cut back on the time you spend with God. Big mistake.

If you've acquired the unfortunate habit of trying to "squeeze" God into the corners of your life, it's time to re-shuffle the items on your to-do list by placing God first. God wants your undivided attention, not the leftovers of your day. And spending time with your Creator is certainly more important than spending time with a few online friends. So, if you haven't already done so, form the habit of spending quality time with the Father. He deserves it . . . and so, for that matter, do you.

Busyness is the great enemy of relationships.

Rick Warren

The foe of opportunity is preoccupation.
Just when God sends along a chance to turn
a great victory for mankind, some of us are too busy
puttering around to notice it.

A. W. Tozer

Are you weak? Weary? Confused? Troubled? Pressured?
How is your relationship with God? Is it held in its place
of priority? I believe the greater the pressure,
the greater your need for time alone with Him.

Kay Arthur

Something to Think About: Do first things first, and keep
your focus on high-priority tasks. And remember this: your
highest priority should be your relationship with God and
His Son.

Choosing to Hang Out with Positive People

Iron sharpens iron, and one man sharpens another.
Proverbs 27:17 Holman CSB

When you hang out with positive people, whether online or in person, you feel better about yourself and your world—when you hang out with negative people, you don't. So here's the question: do you want to feel better about yourself and your circumstances . . . or not? The answer you give should help you determine the friends you choose to make—and keep.

If you're really serious about being an optimistic, upbeat, hope-filled Christian, make sure that your friends feel the same way. Because if you choose to hang out with upbeat people, you'll tend to be an upbeat person, too. But if you hang out with the critics, the cynics, and the naysayers, you'll find yourself become a cynic, too. And life is far too short for that.

The next best thing to being wise oneself
is to live in a circle of those who are.

C. S. Lewis

A friend is one who makes me do my best.

Oswald Chambers

Insomuch as anyone pushes you nearer to God,
he or she is your friend.

Anonymous

Something to Think About: Put peer pressure to work for
you. Make up your mind to hang out with people who will
put pressure on you to become a better person.

Choosing to Take Worship Seriously

*Happy are those who hear the joyful call to worship,
for they will walk in the light of your presence, Lord.*

Psalm 89:15 NLT

You probably take time every day to stay connected with your friends. Do you take time each day to worship your Father in heaven? Or do you wait until Sunday morning to praise Him for His blessings? The answer to this question will, in large part, determine the quality and direction of your spiritual life.

When we worship God every day of our lives, we are blessed. When we fail to worship God, for whatever reason, we forfeit the spiritual gifts that He intends for us.

Every day provides opportunities to put God where He belongs: at the center of our lives. When we do so, we worship Him not only with our words, but also with our deeds, and that's as it should be. For believers, God comes first. Always first.

We're here to be worshipers first and workers only second.
The work done by a worshiper will have eternity in it.

A. W. Tozer

To worship Him in truth means to worship
Him honestly, without hypocrisy, standing open and
transparent before Him.

Anne Graham Lotz

Spiritual worship is focusing all we are on all He is.

Beth Moore

Something to Think About: Worship reminds you of the awesome power of God. So worship Him daily, and allow Him to work through you every day of the week (not just on Sunday).

Trying to See Things from God's Perspective

All I'm doing right now, friends, is showing how these things pertain to Apollos and me so that you will learn restraint and not rush into making judgments without knowing all the facts. It is important to look at things from God's point of view. I would rather not see you inflating or deflating reputations based on mere hearsay.

I Corinthians 4:6 MSG

Sometimes, amid the demands of daily life, we lose perspective. Life seems out of balance, our social connections seem strained, and the pressures of everyday living seem overwhelming. What's needed is a fresh perspective, a restored sense of balance . . . and God.

If we call upon the Lord and seek to see the world through His eyes, He will give us guidance and wisdom and perspective. When we make God's priorities our priorities, He will lead us according to His plan and according to His commandments. God's reality is the ultimate reality. May we live accordingly.

What you see and hear depends a good deal on
where you are standing; it also depends on
what sort of person you are.

C. S. Lewis

The Bible is a remarkable commentary on perspective.
Through its divine message, we are brought face to face
with issues and tests in daily living and how,
by the power of the Holy Spirit, we are enabled
to respond positively to them.

Luci Swindoll

Earthly fears are no fears at all.
Answer the big questions of eternity,
and the little questions of life fall into perspective.

Max Lucado

Something to Think About: Keep life in perspective. Your life is an integral part of God's grand plan. So don't become unduly upset over the minor inconveniences of life, and don't worry too much about today's setbacks—they're temporary.

Placing Holiness Before Happiness

Blessed are those who hunger and thirst for righteousness,
for they will be filled.

Matthew 5:6 NIV

Because you are an imperfect human being, you are not "perfectly" happy—and that's perfectly okay with God. He is far less concerned with your happiness than He is with your holiness.

God continuously reveals Himself in everyday life, but He does not do so in order to make you contented; He does so in order to lead you to His Son. So don't be overly concerned with your current level of happiness; it will change. Be more concerned with the current state of your relationship with Christ: He does not change. And because your Savior transcends time and space, you can be comforted in the knowledge that in the end, His joy will become your joy . . . for all eternity.

Holiness isn't in a style of dress. It's not a matter of rules and regulations. It's a way of life that emanates quietness and rest, joy in family, shared pleasures with friends, the help of a neighbor—and the hope of a Savior.

Joni Eareckson Tada

Holiness is not God's asking us to be "good"; it is an invitation to be "His."

Lisa Bevere

There is no detour to holiness.
Jesus came to the resurrection through the cross, not around it.

Leighton Ford

Something to Think About: God is holy and wants you to be holy. Christ died to make you holy. Make sure that your response to Christ's sacrifice is worthy of Him.

Who's in Your Network?

Iron sharpens iron, and one man sharpens another.

Proverbs 27:17 Holman CSB

Do you want to give anybody and everybody an all-access pass to the backstage of your life? No you don't. Some people don't deserve to know everything about you because they haven't yet earned your trust the old fashioned way: face-to-face. Besides, some folks you'll encounter on the Internet certainly don't have your best interests at heart; in fact, some of these folks may even want to hurt you. And since you can't be sure who is your friend or foe on the Internet, you'd better be careful. Very careful.

So when you're deciding who can have access to your online network, decide carefully. And while you're at it, be sure to build in adequate protection, secure passwords, and strong firewalls between you and the bad guys. In the digital world, you have plenty of ways to protect yourself, but none of them work unless you use them.

We are in a continual battle with the spiritual forces of evil, but we will triumph when we yield to God's leading and call on His powerful presence in prayer.

Shirley Dobson

Christianity isn't a religion about going to Sunday school, potluck suppers, being nice, holding car washes, sending your secondhand clothes off to Mexico—as good as those things might be. This is a world at war.

John Eldredge

Light is stronger than darkness—
darkness cannot "comprehend" or "overcome" it.

Anne Graham Lotz

Social Networking Common Sense: Firewalls serve a very valuable purpose and secure passwords are worth the extra effort. So use them.

The Decision to Be Joyful

Rejoice in the Lord always. I will say it again: Rejoice!
Philippians 4:4 Holman CSB

You can't really get to know God until you genuinely experience God's joy for yourself. It's not enough to hear somebody else talk about being a joyful Christian—you must experience Christ's joy in order to understand it. Does that mean that you'll be a joy-filled believer 24 hours a day, seven days a week, from this moment on? Nope. But it does mean that you can experience God's joy personally, frequently, intensely.

So here's a prescription for better spiritual health: Open the door of your soul to Christ. When you do, He will give you peace and joy . . . heaping helpings of peace and joy.

The good life—the one that truly satisfies—
exists only when we stop wanting a better one.

Charles Swindoll

Rejoice, the Lord is King; Your Lord and King adore!
Rejoice, give thanks and sing and triumph evermore.

Charles Wesley

We all go through pain and sorrow, but the presence of
God, like a warm, comforting blanket, can shield us and
protect us, and allow the deep inner joy to surface,
even in the most devastating circumstances.

Barbara Johnson

Something to Think About: Joy begins with a choice: the
choice to establish a genuine relationship with God and
His Son. As Amy Carmichael correctly observed, "Joy is
not gush; joy is not mere jolliness. Joy is perfect acquies-
cence, acceptance, and rest in God's will, whatever comes."

The Decision to Learn God's Lessons (Sooner Rather than Later)

Listen carefully to wisdom; set your mind on understanding.

Proverbs 2:2 NCV

One way that we learn about God is by learning the lessons that He is trying so desperately to teach us. But when it comes to learning God's lessons, most of us can be quite hardheaded. Why? Because we are, by nature, stubborn creatures; and because we seem destined, at times, to make things hard on ourselves.

As we go about the business of learning life's lessons, we can either do things the easy way or the hard way. The easy way can be summed up as follows: when God tries to teach us something, we learn it . . . the first time! Unfortunately, too many of us learn much more slowly than that.

When we resist God's instruction, He continues to teach, whether we like it or not. Our challenge, then, is to discern God's lessons from the experiences of everyday life. Hopefully, we learn those lessons sooner rather than later because the sooner we do so, the sooner He can move on to the next lesson and the next, and the next . . .

The wonderful thing about God's schoolroom is that
we get to grade our own papers. You see,
He doesn't test us so He can learn how well we're doing.
He tests us so we can discover how well we're doing.

Charles Swindoll

A big difference exists between a head full of knowledge
and the words of God literally abiding in us.

Beth Moore

Social Networking Common Sense: Not all social networking sites are alike. Figure out how different sites work before you decide which sites to join.

Discipline Now

So prepare your minds for service and have self-control.
All your hope should be for the gift of grace that will be yours
when Jesus Christ is shown to you.

I Peter 1:13 NCV

Whether you're texting friends or posting on the Internet, it pays to be disciplined and dignified. Yet sometimes it's hard to be a dignified person. Why? Because you live in a world where many prominent people want you to believe that dignified, self-disciplined behavior is going out of style. But don't kid yourself: self-discipline never goes out of style.

Face facts: Life's greatest rewards aren't likely to fall into your lap. To the contrary, your greatest accomplishments will probably require plenty of work and a heaping helping of self-discipline—which, by the way, is perfectly fine with God. After all, He knows that you're up to the task, and He has big plans for you. God will do His part to fulfill those plans, and the rest, of course, depends upon you.

If one examines the secret behind a championship football team, a magnificent orchestra, or a successful business, the principal ingredient is invariably discipline.

James Dobson

What our Lord said about cross-bearing and obedience is not in fine type. It is in bold print on the face of the contract.

Vance Havner

No horse gets anywhere until he is harnessed. No life ever grows great until it is focused, dedicated, disciplined.

Harry Emerson Fosdick

Something to Think About: A disciplined lifestyle gives you more control: The more disciplined you become, the more you can take control over your life (which, by the way, is far better than letting your life take control over you).

Weaving the Golden Rule into Your Social Network

Therefore, whatever you want others to do for you,
do also the same for them—this is the Law and the Prophets.
Matthew 7:12 Holman CSB

The words of Matthew 7:12 remind us that, as believers in Christ, we are commanded to treat others as we wish to be treated. This commandment is, indeed, the Golden Rule for Christians of every generation.

As Christians, we are instructed to be courteous and compassionate whether we're communicating face-to-face or online. As believers, we are called to be gracious, humble, gentle, and kind. But sometimes, we fall short. Sometimes, amid the busyness and confusion of everyday life, we may neglect to share a kind word or a kind deed. This oversight hurts others, and it hurts us as well.

God intends that we make the conscious choice to treat others with kindness and respect, no matter our circumstances, no matter our emotions. Kindness, therefore, is a choice that we, as Christians, must make many times each day. When we weave the thread of kindness into the very fabric of our social connections, we give a priceless gift to others, and we give glory to the One who gave His life for us. As believers, we must do no less.

Do all the good you can. By all the means you can.
In all the ways you can. In all the places you can.
At all the times you can. To all the people you can.
As long as ever you can.

John Wesley

If we have the true love of God in our hearts,
we will show it in our lives. We will not have to go
up and down the earth proclaiming it.
We will show it in everything we say or do.

D. L. Moody

Social Networking Common Sense: Your social network should be a haven of courtesy and kindness. You and your friends deserve no less.

Establish a Growing Relationship with Jesus

But whoever keeps His word, truly in him the love of God is
perfected. This is how we know we are in Him:
the one who says he remains in Him should
walk just as He walked.

1 John 2:5-6 Holman CSB

When you establish a dynamic relationship with Jesus, you'll feel better about yourself, your future, your social connections, and your world. Jesus has called upon believers of every generation (and that includes you) to follow in His footsteps. And God's Word promises that when you follow in Christ's footsteps, you will learn how to live freely and lightly (Matthew 11:28-30).

Are you dealing with issues of self-confidence, self-esteem, or self-respect? Talk to God about your concerns. He's always available. Are you worried about the future? Be courageous and call upon God. He will protect you. Are you confused? Listen to the quiet voice of your Heavenly Father. He is not a God of confusion. Talk with God; listen to Him; follow His commandments . . . and walk with His Son—starting now, and ending never.

Only by walking with God can we hope
to find the path that leads to life.
John Eldredge

Our responsibility is to feed from Him, to stay close to
Him, to follow Him—because sheep easily go astray—
so that we eternally experience the protection and
companionship of our Great Shepherd
the Lord Jesus Christ.
Franklin Graham

Something to Think About: Think about ways that you can follow Christ—and think about ways you can encourage others to do the same.

Worry Less

Therefore don't worry about tomorrow,
because tomorrow will worry about itself.
Each day has enough trouble of its own.

Matthew 6:34 Holman CSB

Because life is sometimes difficult, and because we have understandable fears about the uncertainty of the future, we worry. At times, we may find ourselves fretting over the countless details of everyday life. We may worry about our relationships, our finances, our health, or any number of potential problems, some large and some small.

If you're a "worrier" by nature, it's probably time to re-think the way that you think! Perhaps you've formed the unfortunate habit of focusing too intently on negative aspects of life while spending too little time counting your blessings. If so, take your worries to God . . . and leave them their. When you do, you'll learn to worry a little less and to trust God a little more—and that's as it should be because God is trustworthy, you are protected, and your future can be intensely bright.

Our fears for today, our worries about tomorrow,
and even the powers of hell can't keep God's love away.

Bill Bright

The busier we are, the easier it is to worry,
the greater the temptation to worry,
the greater the need to be alone with God.

Charles Stanley

Today is mine. Tomorrow is none of my business.
If I peer anxiously into the fog of the future,
I will strain my spiritual eyes so that I will not see
clearly what is required of me now.

Elisabeth Elliott

Something to Think About: Worried about something you said, did, Tweeted, or posted? If you made a mistake yesterday, the day to fix it is today. Then, you won't have to worry about it tomorrow.

Choosing the Direction of Your Thoughts

Finally, brothers, whatever is true, whatever is noble, whatever is right, whatever is pure, whatever is lovely, whatever is admirable—if anything is excellent or praiseworthy—think about such things.

Philippians 4:8 NIV

The Internet wants to direct your thoughts in certain ways, usually in the ways of the world. But God wants you to focus on higher things. How will you direct your thoughts today? Will you obey the words of Philippians 4:8 by dwelling upon those things that are honorable, true, and worthy of praise? Or will you allow your thoughts to be hijacked by the negativity that seems to dominate our troubled world.

Are you fearful, angry, bored, or worried? Are you so preoccupied with the concerns of this day that you fail to thank God for the promise of eternity? Are you confused, bitter, or pessimistic? If so, God wants to have a little talk with you. He wants to remind you of His infinite love and His boundless grace. As you contemplate these things, and as you give thanks for God's blessings, negativity should no longer dominate your day or your life.

Make yourselves nests of pleasant thoughts.

John Ruskin

I became aware of one very important concept
I had missed before: my attitude—not my circumstances—
was what was making me unhappy.

Vonette Bright

Attitude is the mind's paintbrush;
it can color any situation.

Barbara Johnson

Something to Think About: Good thoughts can lead you to some very good places . . . and bad thoughts can lead elsewhere. So guard your thoughts accordingly.

Choosing to Be Generous

Each person should do as he has decided in his heart—
not out of regret or out of necessity,
for God loves a cheerful giver.

2 Corinthians 9:7 Holman CSB

When you chat with your friends on the Internet, are you generous with your praise? And when you deal with folks in person, are you just as generous with your possessions? If you intend to obey God's commandments, you must be. When you give, God looks not only at the quality of your gift, but also at the condition of your heart. If you give generously, joyfully, and without complaint, you obey God's Word. But, if you make your gifts grudgingly, or if the motivation for your gift is selfish, you disobey your Creator, even if you have tithed in accordance with Biblical principles.

Today, take God's commandments to heart and make this pledge: Be a cheerful, generous, courageous giver. The world needs your help, and you need the spiritual rewards that will be yours when you give faithfully, prayerfully, and cheerfully.

I have held many things in my hands,
and I have lost them all; but whatever I have placed in
God's hands, that I still possess.

Martin Luther

The mind grows by taking in,
but the heart grows by giving out.

Warren Wiersbe

When somebody needs a helping hand, he doesn't need
it tomorrow or the next day. He needs it now, and that's
exactly when you should offer to help. Good deeds,
if they are really good, happen sooner rather than later.

Marie T. Freeman

Something to Think About: There is a direct relationship
between generosity and joy—the more you give to others,
the more joy you will experience for yourself.

Pleasing God

*For am I now trying to win the favor of people, or God?
Or am I striving to please people? If I were still trying to
please people, I would not be a slave of Christ.*

Galatians 1:10 Holman CSB

Sometimes, it's very tempting to be a people-pleaser.
But usually, it's the wrong thing to do.

When you worry too much about pleasing on-
line friends or in-person friends, you may not worry enough
about pleasing God. And when you fail to please God, you
inevitably pay a very high price for our mistaken priorities.

Whom will you try to please today: your Creator or
your friends? Your obligation is most certainly not to your
peers or Internet acquaintances whom you don't even really know. Your obligation is to an all-knowing and perfect
God. Trust Him always. Love Him always. Praise Him always. And seek to please Him and only Him. Always.

People who constantly, and fervently, seek the approval
of others live with an identity crisis.
They don't know who they are, and they are
defined by what others think of them.

Charles Stanley

Make God's will the focus of your life day by day.
If you seek to please Him and Him alone,
you'll find yourself satisfied with life.

Kay Arthur

Every day, I find countless opportunities to decide
whether I will obey God and demonstrate my love for
Him or try to please myself or the world system.
God is waiting for my choices.

Bill Bright

Something to Think About: If you are burdened with a
"people-pleasing" personality, outgrow it. Realize that you
can't please all of the people all of the time (including your
dates), nor should you attempt to.

The Choice to Travel in the Light

Then Jesus spoke to them again:
"I am the light of the world. Anyone who follows Me will
never walk in the darkness, but will have the light of life."

John 8:12 Holman CSB

God's Holy Word instructs us that Jesus is, "the way, the truth, and the life" (John 14:6-7). Without Christ, we are as far removed from salvation as the east is removed from the west. And without Christ, we can never know the ultimate truth: God's truth.

Truth is God's way: He commands His believers live in truth, and He rewards those who do so. Jesus is the personification of God's liberating truth, a truth that offers salvation to mankind.

Do you seek to walk with God? Do you seek to feel His presence and His peace? And would you like to take your social network with you? Then you must walk in truth; you must walk in the light; you must walk with the Savior. There is simply no other way.

The Bread of Life never gets stale.

Anonymous

Victory is the result of Christ's life lived out in
the believer. It is important to see that victory, not defeat,
is God's purpose for His children.

Corrie ten Boom

Jesus differs from all other teachers; they reach the ear,
but he instructs the heart; they deal with the outward
letter, but he imparts an inward taste for the truth.

C. H. Spurgeon

Something to Think About: Nobody can find Him for you.
God is searching for you; it's up to you—and you alone—to
open your heart to Him.

Return God's Love by Sharing It

My dear, dear friends, if God loved us like this, we certainly ought to love each other.

1 John 4:11 MSG

God loves you. How will you respond to His love? The Bible clearly defines what your response should be: "You shall love the Lord your God with all your heart, with all your soul, and with all your strength" (Deuteronomy 6:5 NKJV). But you must not stop there. You must also love your neighbor as yourself. Jesus teaches that "On these two commandments hang all the Law and the Prophets" (Matthew 22: 40).

Today, as you meet the demands of everyday living, will you pause long enough to return God's love? And then will you share it? Prayerfully, you will. When you embrace God's love, you are forever changed. When you embrace God's love, you feel differently about yourself, your family, your friends, and your world. When you embrace God's love, you have enough love to keep and enough love to share: enough love for a day, enough love for a lifetime, enough love for all eternity.

He who is filled with love is filled with God Himself.

St. Augustine

Although our actions have nothing to do with gaining our own salvation, they might be used by God to save somebody else! What we do really matters, and it can affect the eternities of people we care about.

Bill Hybels

Have you prayed about your resources lately?
Find out how God wants you to use your time
and your money. No matter what it costs,
forsake all that is not of God.

Kay Arthur

Something to Think About: Be creative: There are many ways to say, "I love you." Find them. Use them. And keep using them.

Choose Your Words Carefully

*But I tell you that men will have to give account on
the day of judgment for every careless word they have spoken.
For by your words you will be acquitted,
and by your words you will be condemned.*

Matthew 12:36-37 NIV

How much value do you place on the words you speak, text, post, or Tweet? Hopefully, you understand that your words have great power . . . because they most certainly do. If your words are encouraging, you can lift others up; if your words are hurtful, you can hold others back.

The Bible makes it clear that "Reckless words pierce like a sword, but the tongue of the wise brings healing" (Proverbs 12:18 NIV). So, if you hope to solve problems instead of starting them, you must measure your words carefully. But sometimes, you'll be tempted to speak first and think second (with decidedly mixed results).

Do you seek to be a source of encouragement to others? Are you a beacon of hope to your friends and family? And, do you seek to be a worthy ambassador for Christ? If so, you must speak words that are worthy of your Savior. So avoid angry outbursts. Refrain from impulsive outpourings. Terminate tantrums. Instead, speak words of encouragement and hope to a world that desperately needs both.

When you talk, choose the very same words that you would use if Jesus were looking over your shoulder. Because He is.

Marie T. Freeman

The things that we feel most deeply we ought to learn to be silent about, at least until we have talked them over thoroughly with God.

Elisabeth Elliot

Something to Think About: Cool off before you spout off: If you're too angry to have a conversation that is both loving and constructive, put things on hold until you simmer down.

Aim High

I can do everything through him that gives me strength.
Philippians 4:13 NIV

Are you willing to dream big dreams? Hopefully so; after all, God promises that we can do "all things" through Him. Yet most of us, even the most devout among us, live far below our potential. We take half measures; we dream small dreams; we waste precious time and energy on the distractions of the world. But God has other plans for us. Our Creator intends that we live faithfully, hopefully, courageously, and abundantly. He knows that we are capable of so much more; and He wants us to do the things we're capable of doing; and He wants us to start doing those things now.

You cannot out-dream God.

John Eldredge

Always stay connected to people and seek out
things that bring you joy.
Dream with abandon. Pray confidently.

Barbara Johnson

Set goals so big that unless God helps you,
you will be a miserable failure.

Bill Bright

Something to Think About: Making your dreams come true
requires work. John Maxwell writes "The gap between your
vision and your present reality can only be filled through
a commitment to maximize your potential." Enough said.

Choosing to Avoid the Trap of Perfectionism

Those who wait for perfect weather will never plant seeds;
those who look at every cloud will never harvest crops.
Plant early in the morning, and work until evening,
because you don't know if this or that will succeed.
They might both do well.

Ecclesiastes 11:4,6 NCV

The Internet is full of images and messages that attempt to tell you how you should dress, how much you should weigh, and how to have "fun." Unfortunately, most of these messages are false. You don't have to be "perfect" (by the standards of the Internet) to be perfectly wonderful.

If you find yourself bound up by the chains of perfectionism, it's time to ask yourself who you're trying to impress, and why. If you're trying to impress other people, it's time to reconsider your priorities. Your first responsibility is to the Heavenly Father who created you and to His Son who saved you. Then, you bear a powerful responsibility to your family. But, when it comes to meeting society's unrealistic expectations, forget it!

Remember that when you accepted Christ as your Savior, God accepted you for all eternity. Now, it's your turn to accept yourself and your loved ones. When you do, you'll feel a tremendous weight being lifted from your shoulders. After all, pleasing God is simply a matter of obeying His commandments and accepting His Son. But as for pleasing everybody else? That's impossible!

What makes a Christian a Christian is not perfection but forgiveness.

Max Lucado

The greatest destroyer of good works is the desire to do great works.

C. H. Spurgeon

Social Networking Common Sense: If you have time to text and time to Tweet, you have time to pray, too.

The Decision to Celebrate Life

This is the day the Lord has made;
let us rejoice and be glad in it.

Psalm 118:24 Holman CSB

What is the best day to celebrate life? This one! Today and every day should be a time for celebration as we consider the Good News of God's gift: salvation through Jesus Christ.

What do you expect from the day ahead? Are you expecting God to do wonderful things, or are you living beneath a cloud of worry and doubt?

The familiar words of Psalm 118:24 remind us of a profound yet simple truth: God made this day . . . and we, as believers, should rejoice in His marvelous creation. For Christians, every day begins and ends with God and His Son. Christ came to this earth to give us abundant life and eternal salvation. We give thanks to our Maker when we treasure each day. So with no further delay, let the celebration begin!

Allow your dreams a place in your prayers and plans.
God-given dreams can help you move into
the future He is preparing for you.

Barbara Johnson

Some of us seem so anxious about avoiding hell
that we forget to celebrate our journey toward heaven.

Philip Yancey

Praise and thank God for who He is
and for what He has done for you.

Billy Graham

Something to Think About: If you don't feel like celebrating, start counting your blessings. Before long, you'll realize that you have plenty of reasons to celebrate.

Be Patient and Trust God

Trust in him at all times, O people;
pour out your hearts to him, for God is our refuge.

Psalm 62:8 NIV

The digital world moves fast. But here in the real world, good things usually take time . . . yet most of us don't want to wait. Most of us are impatient for God to grant us the desires of our heart. Usually, we know what we want, and we know precisely when we want it: right now, if not sooner. But God may have other plans. And when God's plans differ from our own, we must trust in His infinite wisdom and in His infinite love.

As busy people living in a fast-paced world, many of us find that waiting quietly for God is difficult. Why? Because we are imperfect human beings seeking to live according to our own timetables, not God's. In our better moments, we realize that patience is not only a virtue, but it is also a commandment from the Creator.

God instructs us to be patient in all things. We must be patient with our families, with our friends, and with our acquaintances. We must also be patient with our Heavenly

Father as He unfolds His plan for our lives. And that's as it should be. After all, think how patient God has been with us.

> He that trusts in his own understanding proves
> that he has no understanding.
>
> C. H. Spurgeon

> There is no place for faith if we expect God to fulfill
> immediately what he promises.
>
> John Calvin

Something to Think About: God has very big plans in store for your life, so trust Him and wait patiently for those plans to unfold. And remember: God's timing is best, so don't allow yourself to become discouraged if things don't work out exactly as you wish. Instead of worrying about your future, entrust it to God.

Seek Fellowship

Then all the people went away to eat and drink, to send some of their food to others, and to celebrate with great joy. They finally understood what they had been taught.

Nehemiah 8:12 NCV

The digital world can be a great way to stay in touch with fellow believers. And that's great because fellowship with other believers should be an integral part of your everyday life. You association with other Christians should be uplifting, enlightening, encouraging, and consistent.

Are you an active member of your own fellowship? Are you a builder of bridges inside the four walls of your church and outside it? Do you contribute to God's glory by contributing your time and your talents to a close-knit band of believers? Hopefully so. The fellowship of believers is intended to be a powerful tool for spreading God's Good News and uplifting His children. And God intends that you be a fully contributing member of that fellowship. Your intentions should be the same.

One of the ways God refills us after failure is through the blessing of Christian fellowship. Just experiencing the joy of simple activities shared with other children of God can have a healing effect on us.

Anne Graham Lotz

The Bible knows nothing of solitary religion.

John Wesley

Christians are like coals of a fire.
Together they glow—apart they grow cold.

Anonymous

Something to Think About: Christians shouldn't try to be Lone Rangers. We are members of a spiritual family, and we need one another. Are you trying to be a Lone Ranger? If so, it's time to form a posse made up of faithful, God-fearing friends.

The Decision to Overcome Pessimism

Cast your burden on the Lord, and He will support you;
He will never allow the righteous to be shaken.

Psalm 55:22 Holman CSB

Some chat rooms are loaded with cynics, skeptics, and pessimists. But if you're ever tempted to go negative, remember this: Pessimism and Christianity don't mix. Why? Because Christians have every reason to be optimistic about life here on earth and life eternal. As C. H. Spurgeon observed, "Our hope in Christ for the future is the mainstream of our joy." But sometimes, we fall prey to worry, frustration, anxiety, or sheer exhaustion, and our hearts become heavy. What's needed is plenty of rest, a large dose of perspective, and God's healing touch, but not necessarily in that order.

Today, make this promise to yourself and keep it: vow to be a hope-filled Christian. Think optimistically about your life, your profession, your future, and your students. Trust your hopes, not your fears. Take time to celebrate God's glorious creation. And then, when you've filled your heart with hope and gladness, share your optimism with others. They'll be better for it, and so will you. But not necessarily in that order.

A pessimist is someone who believes that
when her cup runneth over she'll need a mop.
Barbara Johnson

He who is his own guide is guided by a fool.
C. H. Spurgeon

Never yield to gloomy anticipation.
Place your hope and confidence in God.
He has no record of failure.
Mrs. Charles E. Cowman

Something to Think About: If you genuinely believe that God is good and that His Son died for your sins, how can you be pessimistic about your future? The answer, of course, is that you can't!

Choosing to Manage Your Time Wisely

We can't afford to waste a minute, must not squander these precious daylight hours in frivolity and indulgence, in sleeping around and dissipation, in bickering and grabbing everything in sight. Get out of bed and get dressed! Don't loiter and linger, waiting until the very last minute. Dress yourselves in Christ, and be up and about!

Romans 13:13-14 MSG

Social networking takes time. But it's up to you to make sure that it doesn't take up too much time.

Time is a nonrenewable gift from God. But sometimes, we treat our time here on earth as if it were not a gift at all: We may be tempted to invest our lives in trivial pursuits and mindless diversions. But our Father in heaven wants us to do more . . . much more.

Are you one of those people who puts things off until the last minute? Do you waste time doing things that don't matter very much while putting off the important things until it's too late to do the job right? If so, it's now time to start making better choices.

It may seem like you've got all the time in the world to do the things you need to do, but time is shorter than you think. Time here on earth is limited . . . use it or lose it.

To choose time is to save time.
Francis Bacon

The more time you give to something,
the more you reveal its importance and value to you.
Rick Warren

Frustration is not the will of God.
There is time to do anything and everything
that God wants us to do.
Elisabeth Elliot

Something to Think About: Every day, you get to choose how you will spend your time. If you choose wisely, you'll improve yourself and your life.

Choosing the Positive Path

But the path of the just is like the shining sun, that shines ever brighter unto the perfect day. The way of the wicked is like darkness; they do not know what makes them stumble.

Proverbs 4:18-19 NKJV

When Jesus addressed His disciples, He warned that each one must, "take up his cross and follow me." The disciples must have known exactly what the Master meant. In Jesus' day, prisoners were forced to carry their own crosses to the location where they would be put to death. Thus, Christ's message was clear: in order to follow Him, Christ's disciples must deny themselves and, instead, trust Him completely. Nothing has changed since then.

If we are to be dutiful disciples of the One from Galilee, we must trust Him and we must follow Him. Jesus never comes "next." He is always first. He shows us the path of life.

Do you seek to be a worthy disciple of Jesus? Then pick up His cross today and follow in His footsteps. When you do, you can walk with confidence: He will never lead you astray.

God's promises aren't celestial life preservers that
He throws out to strangers in the storm. They are
expressions of His love and care, given to His children
who walk with Him and seek to obey Him.

Warren Wiersbe

You can't walk with God and hold hands
with Satan at the same time.

Anonymous

Be such a person, and live such a life, that if every person
were such as you, and every life a life like yours,
this earth would be God's Paradise.

Phillips Brooks

Something to Think About: Growing to spiritual maturity
requires a plan. What is yours?

Choosing to Let God Transform Your Life

*Your old life is dead. Your new life, which is your real life—
even though invisible to spectators—
is with Christ in God. He is your life.*

Colossians 3:3 MSG

Has your relationship with Jesus transformed you into an extremely different person? Hopefully so! Otherwise, you're missing out on the joy and abundance that can be yours through Christ.

Think, for a moment, about the "old" you, the person you were before you invited Christ to reign over your heart. Now, think about the "new" you, the person you've become since then. Is there a difference between the "old" version of you and the "new-and-improved" version? There should be! And that difference should be evident to you, to your family, and to your friends.

When you invited Christ to reign over your heart, you become a radically new creation. This day offers yet another opportunity to behave yourself like that new person. When you do, God will guide your steps and bless your endeavors . . . forever.

Are you willing to make radical changes for Jesus? If so, you may be certain of this fact: He's standing at the door of your heart, patiently waiting to form an extreme, life-altering relationship with you.

Believe and do what God says.
The life-changing consequences will be limitless,
and the results will be confidence and peace of mind.
Franklin Graham

If you'll flip from cover to cover, you'll notice that
it's overwhelmingly a book of stories—
tales of men and women who walked with God.
John Eldredge

Something to Think About: A true conversion experience results in a life transformed by Christ and a commitment to following in His footsteps.

The Ultimate Choice

For God so loved the world that He gave
His only begotten Son, that whoever believes in Him
should not perish but have everlasting life.

John 3:16 NKJV

Everything in this world, including everything contained in the digital world, is time-limited. All these things will pass. But wait, there's more!

God offers you the gift of eternal life. Eternal life is not an event that begins when you die. Eternal life begins when you invite Jesus into your heart right here on earth. So it's important to remember that God's plans for you are not limited to the ups and downs of everyday life. If you've allowed Jesus to reign over your heart, you've already begun your eternal journey.

Today, give praise to the Creator for His priceless gift, the gift of eternal life. And then, when you've offered Him your thanks and your praise, share His Good News with all who cross your path.

God loves you and wants you to experience
peace and life—abundant and eternal.

Billy Graham

If you are a believer, your judgment will not
determine your eternal destiny. Christ's finished work on
Calvary was applied to you the moment you
accepted Christ as Savior.

Beth Moore

In his life, Christ is an example showing us how to live;
in his death, he is a sacrifice satisfying for our sins.

Martin Luther

Something to Think About: The ultimate choice for you
is the choice to invite God's Son into your heart. Choose
wisely . . . and immediately.